THE
HISTORY
OF
BUKHARA

THE
HISTORY
OF
BUKHARA

*Translated from the
Persian Abridgement of the Arabic
Original by Narshakhi*

Richard N. Frye

 Markus Wiener Publishers
Princeton

For information write to:
Markus Wiener Publishers
231 Nassau Street, Princeton, NJ 08542
www.markuswiener.com

Cover design: Noah Wiener

Appendixes II and III were originally published in *Bukhara: The Myth
and the Architecture*, Attilio Petruccioli, ed., Aga Khan Program for
Islamic Architecture at Harvard University and the Massachusetts
Institute of Technology, Cambridge, 1999. Reprinted by permission.

Library of Congress Cataloging-in-Publication Data
    Narshakhi, Abā Bakr Muhammad ibn Ja'far, 899-959.
    [Ta 'rikh Bukhara. English]
  The history of Bukhara / translated from the Persian abridgement
of the Arabic original by Narshakhi ; [edited and translated by]
Richard N. Frye.
    p. cm.
    Includes bibliographical references.
    ISBN-13: 978-1-55876-418-7 (hardcover : alk. paper)
    ISBN-13: 978-1-55876-419-4 (paperback : alk paper)
    1. Bukhoro (Uzbekistan)—History. I. Frye, Richard Nelson, 1920– .
II. Title.
    DK949.5.B85N3713 2006
    958.7—dc22
    2006029703

Markus Wiener Publishers books are printed in the United States of
America on acid-free paper, and meet the guidelines for permanence
and durability of the Committee on Production Guidelines for Book
Longevity of the Council on Library Resources.

To Nels of the future

Table of Contents

Preface

The *History of Bukhara* is a companion volume to Ibn Fadlan's account of his trip to the Volga river, inasmuch as both deal with Central Asia in the tenth century. The former is translated from Persian and the latter from Arabic, but both give impressions of the age of the Samanid dynasty which ruled a vast area over eastern Iran and Central Asia. These are also primary sources, and even though not free from errors and even fancy, they give the reader and student a picture of the ideas and impressions of two authors of the time. From both we learn about the importance of Khwarazm as a center of trade with the people of the steppes, as well as a flourishing agricultural and crafts region. This contrasts with the sorry condition of the area around the Aral Sea today. From both we learn of the spread of Islam and the efforts of missionaries among the Turkic tribes of Central Asia. They complement each other in remarks about the brilliant civilization of Central Asia, long an almost *terra incognita*, not only for the West but also for the western Islamic world.

The *History of Bukhara*, however, tells much more, such as the coming of the Arabs to Central Asia and the important role of the city of Bukhara in contributions by its scholars to the ecumenical culture of Islam which reached an apex from the tenth to twelfth centuries of our era. It is important to read and study original sources, as well as modern accounts, to obtain a better conception of a time and place as seen by contemporaries.

I find it is fitting that I began with Bukhara and end with Bukhara.

Introduction

The Book

In 1953 my translation of Narshakhi's *History of Bukhara* was published by the Mediaeval Academy of America, but after a few years it was out of print. Markus Wiener, head of the publishing house of the same name, encouraged me to reissue the work for students and the general reader without the sometimes pedantic notes. Likewise, diacritical marks for words and names in the text should be omitted, since readers unfamiliar with the Arabic alphabet would not need them, while others would understand what the originals were. Instead of the notes, I added a commentary to the text. Variant readings also were not included in my readings of the history. The reader should refer to the Persian text by Mudaris Rizavi for information in regard to variant readings, and also about the historical personalities in the book.

After translating the text years ago, I wanted to make a definitive edition of the Persian text but realized that access to the many manuscripts in the Soviet Union was necessary, which led to my trip there in 1955. In Leningrad I learned that Olga Ivanova Smirnova at the Oriental Institute of the Academy of

Sciences intended to make an edition of the text. I gave her my films of the manuscript in the library of the American Oriental Society at Yale Unniversity, of another ms. in the British Museum and a third one in the Royal Asiatic Society in London. Since the book was popular in Central Asia, many manuscripts of the work existed in various libraries of the Soviet Union. In addition to the manuscripts listed in my 1953 book, five more manuscripts were found in Dushanbe, Tajikistan when I lived there in 1991–2. Unfortunately, Olga Ivanova died without completing her work. I hope that someone will continue her project, for I am too old and weary to embark again on such a task.

Abu Bakr Muhammad ibn Ja'far ibn Zakariya ibn Khattab ibn Sharikh al-Narshakhi (ca. 286/899–348/960), from the village of Narshakh near the city of Bukhara, wrote his history in Arabic and presented it to the Samanid ruler Nuh ibn Nasr in 332/943. Nothing more is known about Narshakhi and this was the only book he wrote. It was translated into Persian by Abu Nasr Ahmad ibn Muhammd ibn Nasr al-Qubavi in 522/1128 who added items from his own time, as well as adding passages from other works, especially the *Khaza'in al-'Ulum* (treasury of the sciences) of a certain otherwise unknown Abu'l- Hasan 'Abd al-Rahman ibn Muhammad al-Nishapuri. He omitted some passages of the original and brought the history down to 365/975. In 574/1178 Muhammad ibn Zufar ibn'Umar abridged the Persian text and presented it to the religious head of the Hanefite law school in Bukhara. The latter had the honorary title Sadr al-Sudur (chief judge) whose name was 'Abd al-'Aziz ibn Burhan al-Din, and who also was governor of Bukhara for the Qara Khitay rulers of that region of Central Asia. Other than their mention here we have no information about the translator or abridger of the volume.

An unknown author added to the text after the time of the Mongol conquest of the city in 616/1219, since in Chapters VIII and XVI we find mention of the Mongol conquest of Bukhara. Thus the text which we have has been translated, abridged and increased by a number of emendators.

It is difficult to know what sources Narshakhi used in his writing; probably, as most authors of local histories of his time, he was concerned with the history Muslim jurists, scholars and writers who lived in Bukhara. It is unknown who, author, translator or abridger of his work, used two authors, Muhammad ibn Salih al-Laithi and Abu 'l-Hasan Mada'ini, in the account of the rise of the Samanids. The latter author, whose writings have not survived, was the main source of information about the Arab conquest of Central Asia used by Tabari and other authors. Al-Laithi is an unknown author. Muhammad ibn Zufar ibn 'Umar, who added items on the pre-Islamic history of Bukhara, derived that information mainly from the book called the *Khaza'in al-'Ulum*, mentioned above.

For his account of the false prophet Muqanna', Narshakhi mentions Tabari and an unknown author, Ibrahim, as his sources of information. Although Narshakhi's historical account finds parallels in other books, such as Tabari, Atham al-Kufi, and others, some of his information is unique, but must be used with care to determine its reliability.

Anyone interested in details of past publications of Narshakhi's history may refer to my translation of 1953. In our remarkable new world of the Internet the reader will find ample accounts of the life and times of our author; consequently I have refrained from burdening this translation with an extensive bibliography or detailed information about Bukhara or the Samanids. On the other hand, I hope to place Bukhara in the milieu and time of ninth and tenth century Central Asia, and to elucidate passages in Narshakhi's book. At the outset, however, the following general remarks hopefully will help the reader to place our history of Bukhara in a wide perspective. In this translation, words or phrases enclosed by [ ] marks indicate additions from a manuscript of the text other than the majority of manuscripts. And ( ) marks indicate additions to the text for better understanding, while < > adds pious remarks about various people.

The Time

By the end of the third century of the Hejira (about 900 Common Era) Central Asia had been under Muslim rule for more than two centuries, and as part of the extensive 'Abbasid Caliphate, for one-and-a-half centuries. There remained pockets of Zoroastrians, Christians and Shamanists in isolated villages of Central Asia, however, Islam had spread everywhere, although in the principal town, formerly called Numijkath, but now itself Bukhara, one could find followers of the various faiths mentioned above, for the old spirit of tolerance was still to be found in Central Asia. In the oases of Central Asia, trade and commerce also continued to flourish as in pre-Islamic times. Then, and under Islam as well, a relaxed attitude towards religion existed. Not that fanatics or variant forms of Islam, considered heretical by the state, were absent, but they were minority voices in the populace. The oases of Bukhara, Samarqand, Chach (Shash or present Tashkent), and others, had been stepping off bases for *Ghazis* (fighters for the faith), who sought to spread Islam among the Turkic tribes, and in the tenth century this activity of missionaries continued but on a reduced scale, less sponsored by the state and more a private enterprise.

The Muslim conquerors in Central Asia for the most part left local rulers in place to collect taxes and handle local affairs for the Arab army commanders. In Bukhara there was a local dynasty called Jamuk or Chao wu in Chinese sources, probably a clan or family name. From inscriptions on silver plates and coins, and from Arabic sources, we can tentatively reconstruct the sequence of local rulers or *xwabo* (γωβω in Sogdian), which was interpreted as *khudah* in Arabic sources. The earliest ruler of the oasis of Bukhara of whom we have evidence was Kana, or Kawa, whose name, it seems, appears on the earliest coins of a type copied after the Sasanian silver coins of Bahram IV (see below). Then we have Bidun who died about 683, or earlier, and was followed by his widow Khutak Khatun, who ruled until ca. 689. I follow the reconstruction of Aleksandr Naymark

(Naymark, 2004), who gives cogent reasons for identifying the ruler Khunuk as a usurper, who may be identified as the lord, *xwabo*, of the town of Vardana in the Bukharan oasis. He seems to have controlled Bukhara for twenty years, to judge from the extent of his coins. Unfortunately the sources are confused about events of this period and we must conjecture the sequence of events and rule. In any case, by the grace of Qutaiba, Tughshada ibn Bidun regained control of Bukhara about 709 and ruled until 738 when he was killed. It is possible that there were two rulers, father and son, with the same name during this long period, but this is unlikely. Then Tughshada's son Qutaiba ibn Tughshada ruled from 738 to 751 when he was killed by order of Abu Muslim the 'Abbasid general. The following succession is unclear, for Qutaiba ibn Tughshada was followed by either one brother Sukan, who may have ruled from 750 to 757, or more likely by another brother Bunyat ibn Tughshada, who held office until 782 when he was killed by order of the Caliph al-Mahdi, and the authority of the local rulers was effectively ended. Narshakhi's account is confused and other sources are no better. Abrui or Abarzi is mentioned as the first ruler of Bukhara by our author, but he is only known from this source, Another ruler of Bukhara was Dizo(y), whose name appears on a silver dish, but whose time of rule is unknown, probably earlier than those mentioned above. Although the dates, and even sequence of rulers, are uncertain, the real authority rested in the hands of the Muslim conquerors after the time of Qutaiba.

The oasis of Bukhara had many settlements, as reported by Narshakhi's work and by Arabic geography books, and for some time in the pre-Islamic period the town of Paikand was the most important center. Then the town of Numijkath, at the site where the river Zarafshan (probably formerly called Nami or Numi) divided into several channels, became important, and the name of the oasis was given to that settlement. In my opinion this was the origin of the city of Bukhara and the reason for its name, even though it originally may have been a folk etymology meaning "lovely" or "glorious" applied to the entire oasis (see below).

Narshakhi gives interesting details about the conquest of the city by the Muslims and the establishment of the religion of Islam there. For example, he gives two Sogdian words, used instead of Arabic, to signal to converts that they should bend down in prayer. It suggests that Arabic phrases were translated into Sogdian so the natives could understand the rituals of the new faith. So our book has more information about its city than other histories of towns, which, like the histories of Nishapur, are only lists of prominent religious leaders or scholars, almost like an address or phone book.

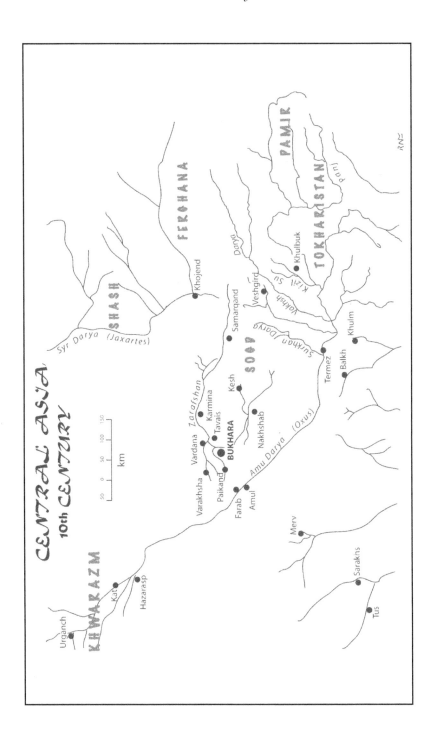

CENTRAL ASIA
10th CENTURY

KHWARAZM
Urganch
Kat'
Hazarasp

SHASH
Syr Darya (Jaxartes)
Khojend

FERGHANA

PAMIR

TOKHARISTAN
Khulbuk

Panj
Kizil Su
Vakhsh
Danya
Veshgird
Samarqand
SOGD
Kesh
Surkhan Darya
Termez
Balkh
Khulm

Zarafshan
Vardana
Karmina
Tavais
Varakhsha
BUKHARA
Paikand
Nakhshab
Farab
Amul
Amu Darya (Oxus)

Merv

Sarakhs
Tus

50 0 50 100 150
km

THE
HISTORY
OF
BUKHARA

The Translation

The History of Bukhara

I

Introduction

Thanks and praise be to God the most high exalted be His glory, who is the creator of the world and the knower of hidden things. He is the daily provider for living creatures and the keeper of heaven and earth. Blessing and benediction be on the Chosen of Men, the Seal of the Prophets, Muhammad the Elect, <God bless him and his family, companions, followers and partisans. May God's favor be upon all of them.>

Abu Nasr Ahmad ibn Muhammad ibn Nasr al-Qubavi says that Abu Bakr Muhammad ibn Jafar al-Narshakhi had composed a book dedicated to the amir Hamid (the exalted) abu Muhammad Nuh ibn Nasr ibn Ahmad ibn Isma'il al-Samani

(331–343/943–54,) <may God the Exalted show mercy on him>, containing an account of Bukhara, its qualities and excellencies, and of what is in it and its villages of incomes and profits, and of anything which has any relation to it. It is also an account of the traditions on the superior qualities of Bukhara, which have come from the Prophet, <may God bless him and give him peace>, and from his companions, followers, and the learned men of religion, <may the favor of God be on them all>.

This book was written in Arabic in an elegant style during the months of the year 332/943. Since most people do not show a desire to read an Arabic book, friends of mine requested me to translate the book into Persian. I consented (and) translated (the book) in Jumada 'l-'Ula of the year 522 (May 1128). Whenever unimportant items were mentioned in the Arabic manuscript, by the reading of which the temper became more fatigued, an account of such things was not made. In the year 574/1178 the least of slaves, Muhamrnad ibn Zufar ibn 'Umar read an abridgement of the work to the exalted assembly of the chief minister of the world, Khwaja Imam, the most glorious, most honored, proof of the nation and the religion, sword of Islam and the Muslims, scimitar of the Imams in the two worlds, lord of the religious law, backbone of the caliphate, and chief of the holy places (Mecca and Medina), mufti of the two horizons, noble on both sides (father and mother), possessor of virtues and glories, 'Abd al-Aziz ibn al-Sadr al-Imam al-Hamid Burhan al-Din 'Abd al-'Aziz, <God consecrate the souls of his ancestors, and bless in this life his posterity in honor and glory>.

II

An account of the group
who were judges in Bukhara

There was Sibavaih ibn 'Abd al-'Aziz al-Bukhari the grammarian. Muhammad ibn A'yan said, "I heard from 'Abdallah (ibn) Mubarak that when Sibavaih filled the office of judge in Bukhara he did not do any injustice (even to the amount of) two *dirhams.*" He then asserted, "Two *dirhams* is too much, he did not do an atom of injustice (to anyone)."

Mukhallad ibn 'Umar was also a judge for many years, and at the end of his service he became a martyr. Another was Abu Daim Hazim Sadusi, whom the caliph appointed as judge. Another was 'Isa ibn Musa al-Taimi, known as Ghunjar <God show mercy on him> who, when the appointment was proffered him, did not accept it. The sultan ordered, "If you will not accept it, select another person to whom we should give it." This he also did not accept. The sultan ordered a list of people (suitable for the appointment) of judge to be read to him. So they did, and when they mentioned each name to him, he said, "He should not be appointed." When the name of Hasan ibn 'Uthman Hamadani was mentioned he remained silent. They concluded that silence from him was a sign of agreement, so Hasan ibn 'Uthman was appointed judge. During his term of office there was no one in the cities of Khurasan who equalled him in knowledge and piety. After him there was 'Amir ibn 'Umar ibn 'Imran, then Isbaq ibn Ibrahim ibn al-Khaita. After his replacement, the latter died in Tus in the year 208/823.

Another (judge) was Sa'id ibn Khalaf al-Balkhi who was appointed at the end of Jumada 'l-'Ula of the year 213 (July 828). He fulfilled the function of a judge in such a manner that he was set up as an example of impartiality, justice, and kindness to the people of God the Exalted. He established good customs with impartiality and justice, so that the strong could not tyrannize the weak. Among other things, the dams and the distribution of water in Bukhara were (the results) of his (efforts). Another was 'Abd al-Majid ibn Ibrahim al-Narshakhi <God have mercy on him>. They said he belonged to the company of pious men. Another was Ahmad ibn Ibrahim al-Barkadi <God have mercy on him> who was a judge in the time of the sultan Ahmad ibn Isma'il al-Samani. He was both a jurist and an ascetic. Another was Abu Dharr Muhammad ibn Yusuf al-Bukhari, who was one of the followers of Imam Shafi'i <may God have mercy on him>. He was learned and pious and he was given precedence among the learned men of Bukhara. He was tested many times with secret bribes in every way, but in no wise did he degrade himself, rather day by day his righteousness and sense of justice grew more evident. When he became old he asked for a release from the office of judge. He then went on the pilgrimage (to Mecca). He finished the pilgrimage and stayed some time in 'Iraq where he was busy in the investigation of the traditions of the Prophet <may God bless him and give him peace>. He studied and then returned to Bukhara, and chose a life of retirement till the time of his death. <May God show mercy on him.>

Another was Abu Fadl ibn Muhammad ibn Ahmad al-Marvazi al-Sulami the jurist. He was the author of the book *Mukhtasar-i kafi*, and a judge for many years in Bukhara. In his service he was never reproached an iota. He showed justice and impartiality to all, so that in his time he did not have a rival in the world in learning and piety. Afterwards he became the prime minister of the sultan. He died and became a martyr.

The author of this book says that if we mention all of the learned men of Bukhara it would require volumes. The group, which we have mentioned, is among those of whom the Prophet said, "The learned men of my faith are (equal) to the prophets of the sons of Isra'il."

Muhammad ibn Ja'far al-Narshakhi has not put the following section in his book, but Abu'l-Hasan 'Abd al-Rahman Muhammad al-Nishapuri has mentioned it in the book "The Treasury of the Sciences." This place, which today is Bukhara, was (formerly) a swamp; part of it was a bed of reeds and part planted with trees and a meadow. Some places were such that no animal could find footing there, because the snows melted on the mountains of the districts about Samarqand and the water collected there. In the vicinity of Samarqand is a large valley (in which) is a river called Masaf. A great quantity of water would collect in that river, and the water would dig away much earth and carry down much mud so these hollows would be filled. Much water used to flow by carrying the mud till it reached Bitik and Farab where the water was diverted. The area, which is Bukhara, was filled and the land became level. That (river) became the great river of Sughd, and the filled area became Bukhara. People gathered from all sides and were happy there. Some people came from Turkistan, for there was much water, many trees, and plenty of game here. They were pleased with this area and settled down. They first set up tents and pavilions where they dwelled, but in time more people assembled and they erected buildings. Their number increased and they chose one whom they made amir. His name was Abrui. The city (of Bukhara) did not yet exist, but there were several villages. Among them were Nur, Kharqan Rud, Vardana, Taravcha, Safna, and Isvana. The large settlement where the ruler lived was Baikand, but the town was Qal'ai Dabusi, which was called "his city." After the lapse of some time, as Abrui grew powerful he exercised tyranny such that the inhabitants of the district could not stand it. The *dihqans* and the rich (merchants) fled from this district and went to Turkistan and Taraz where they built a city. They called the city Jamukat because the great *dihqan*, who was chief of the band which had fled, was called *Jamuk*. In the language of Bukhara *jamuk* means a jewel, and *kat* means city, i.e. the city of the jewel. In the language of Bukhara a noble is called *Jamuk*, i.e. such a person is a jewel. Then those people who had remained in Bukhara sent a man to their nobles and asked for succor from the oppression of Abrui. Those nobles and *dihqans* went to the ruler of the Turks who was called Qara Jurin Turk and because of his size had been nicknamed Biyaghu. They asked him for assistance. Biyaghu sent his son, who was called Shir-i Kishvar, with a large army. When Shir-i Kishvar came to Bukhara he seized Abrui in Baikand and imprisoned him. He ordered a large sack filled with red bees, and they confined Abrui in that sack until he died.

This district so pleased Shir-i Kishvar that he sent his father a letter asking for (the governorship) of this area, for he wanted permission to remain in Bukhara. An answer came from Biyaghu, "I give this district to you." Shiri Kishvar sent a person to Jamukat to those people who had fled from Bukhara, in order to bring them back with their wives and children to Bukhara. Then it was promulgated that whosoever returned from Jamukat would become one of the aristocracy. (This was) because whoever had been rich or a *dihqan* had fled while the mendicants and poor had remained. When that group returned, the people who had remained destitute became servants of the former. Among those nobles was a great dihqan called Bukhar Khudah, for he was of an old *dihqan* family, and his estates were more (than others). The greater part of these (poor) people were his peasants and servants. Shir-i Kishvar built the city proper of Bukhara and the villages of Mamastin, Saqmatin, Samatin and Farab. He ruled twenty years and after him there was another ruler who built Iskijkat, Shargh and Ramitin. After that the village of Farakhsha was founded. When the daughter of the king of *Chin* was brought to Bukhara as a bride, a pagoda (*but-khana*) was brought from *Chin* in her trousseau. This pagoda was placed in Ramitin.

In the time of the caliphate of the Amir of the Faithful Abu Bart al-Sadiq (632–4) <may God be pleased with him>, coins of pure silver were struck in Bukhara. Previous (to this time) there had been no coinage in Bukhara.

In the reign of Mu'awiya (661–680) Bukhara (*sic*) was conquered by Qutaiba ibn Muslim, and Tughshada became its ruler. He ruled thirty-two years on the part of Qutaiba ibn Muslim. It was in the time of Nasr ibn Saiyar, who was the amir of Khurasan, (738–748) that Abu Muslim killed him (Tughshada) in Samarqand (*sic*). Tughshada ruled ten years after Qutaiba and Abu Muslim <may God show him mercy> killed him. After him his brother Sukan ibn Tughshada ruled seven years. He was killed in the palace of Farakhsha on the order of the caliph. A quarrel arose and he was killed in his own palace in the month of Ramadan. A booklet was lying on his lap and he was reading the Qur'an when they killed him. They buried him in the (same) palace yard. After him his brother Bunyat ibn Tughshada ruled seven years and was killed in the palace of Farakhsha at the command of the caliph. The reason for that will be mentioned later. Afterwards Bukhara was in the hands of the children of Tughshada, his servants and grandchildren, until the time of the amir Isma'il Samani, who took the kingdom from the descendants of Bukhar Khudah. An account of that will be mentioned later.

III

An account of the Khatun, who was the ruler of Bukhara, and of her children who ruled after her

Muhammad ibn Ja'far says that when Bidun Bukhar Khudah died there remained a suckling son named Tughshada. Khatun, who was the mother of the boy, became ruler and reigned for fifteen years. During her reign the Arabs began to come to Bukhara. Each time Khatun made peace and paid them tribute. So it was said that in her time there was no one more capable then she. She governed wisely and the people were obedient to her.

She had the custom every day of coming out of the gate of the fortress of Bukhara on a horse and halting at the gate of the Rigistan, which was called the gate of the "forage sellers." She used to sit on a throne, while before her stood slaves, masters of the seraglio, i.e. the eunuchs, and the nobles. She made it an obligation for the rural population that every day, from the *dihqans* and princes, two hundred youths, girded with gold belts and swords carried (on the shoulder), should appear for service and stand at a distance. When Kharun came out all made obeisance to her and stood in two rows while she inquired into the affairs of state. She issued orders and prohibitions, and gave a robe of honor to whomsoever she wished and punishment to whom she wished. Thus she was seated from early morning to lunchtime. After that she returned to the castle and sent trays, giving food to her entire retinue. When it was evening she came out in the same manner and sat on the throne. Some *dihqans* and princes stood before her in two rows attendance till the sun set. Then she rose, mounted a horse and returned to the palace while the rest went to their homes in the villages. On another day other people would come and be in attendance in the same manner, as many times as a turn came to that group. Every year each group had to come in this manner four days.

When this Khatun died, and her son Tughshada had grown up and was fit to rule, everyone coveted the kingdom. A certain vezir called Vardan Khudah, who ruled the district of Vardana, had come from Turkistan. Qutaiba had to fight many battles against him. Several times he drove him from this district so that he fled to Turkistan. Vardan Khudah died and Qutaiba seized Bukhara. Qutaiba gave Bukhara back to Tughshada and made him ruler. He (Qutaiba) cleared the kiagdom (of sedition) for him and took the power away from all of his enemies. Tughshada accepted the faith (Islam) from Qutaiba and ruled Bukhara as long as Qutaiba was alive. After Qutaiba's death Bukhara was ruled by him thirty-two years till the time of Nasr ibn Saiyar. After his conversion to Islam a son was born to him, and out of friendship he called him Qutaiba. After Tughshada, his son, Qutaiba, sat on the throne. He was a Muslim for a while until he apostatized in the time of Abu Muslim <may God show mercy on him>. Abu Muslim heard (of his apostasy) and killed him. He also killed his brother with his followers.

After that, Bunyat ibn Tughshada became ruler of Bukhara. He had been born into Islam. He was a Muslim for some time until Muqanna' appeared and the revolt of the people in "White Raiments" arose in the rural districts of Bukhara. Bunyat showed partiality for them and gave them help, so the people in "White Raiments" extended their influence and grew in power. The master of the post sent this information to the caliph who was Mahdi, (158–169/775–785). In order to have an end with the affair of Muqanna' and the wearers of "White Raiments" Mahdi sent horsemen. Bunyat was seated in his castle in Farakhsha drinking wine with a company. He looked from an observation post and saw the horsemen from afar, who were rapidly approaching. He suspected that they were coming from the caliph. He was speculating on that when they came and, without speaking a word, drew their swords and cut off his head. This was in the year 166/782 or 3. His company all dispersed and those horsemen returned. When the apostasy of Qutaiba ibn Tughshada became evident, Abu Muslim killed him and gave his servants, estates, and property to his brother Bunyat ibn Tughshada (whose descendants) held them till the time of the amir Isma'il Samani. After Bunyat apostatized and was killed, this property went to the descendants of Bukhar Khudah.

The last person, who (held and then) lost the estates, was Abu Ishaq Ibrahim ibn Khalid ibn Bunyat. Ismail lived in Bukhara and the kingdom was in his hands. Every year he sent part of the harvest of Transoxiana to his brother Nasr whence it was dispatched to the Amir of the Faithful, Muqtadir (*sic*), (295–320/908–932). Amir Isma'il Samani took the estates and property away from him (Abu Ishaq) because Ahmad ibn Muhammad (ibn) Laith, who was chief of police, one day said to the amir, "Oh amir, from whom did Abu Ishaq obtain such fine property, with such a produce?" Amir Isma'il Samani replied, "This is not (really) their property, but the property of the ruler." Ahmad ibn Muhammad (ibn) Laith said "It is rightfully their property, but because of the apostasy of their father the caliph took it from them and has made it the property of the public treasury. But he gave it back to them as a kind of lease and stipend. He (Abu Ishaq) has not rendered service in recompense, but has considered the property as his own." They (the amir and Ahmad) were talking when Abu Ishaq Ibrahim entered. Amir Isma'il Samani said to him, "Oh Abu Ishaq, how much income do you receive each year from your property?" Abu Ishaq answered, "After much trouble and difficulty I re-

ceive 20,000 *dirhams* a year." Amir Isma'il ordered Ahmad ibn
Muhammad (ibn) Laith to take this property and to tell Abul-
Hasan the paymaster to give him 20,000 *dirhams* a year. So the
property passed from his hands and did not return to him. Abu
Ishaq died in the year 301/913 or 14. His descendants have re-
mained in the villages of Safna and Siyavunj.

IV

Bukhara and the places adjoining it

Abu'l-Hasan Nishapuri in the book "The Treasury of the Sciences" has contended that the city of Bukhara, although the Oxus river (*sic*) is in the middle of it, is one of the cities of Khurasan. Karmina is one of the villages of Bukhara, and its water comes from the water of Bukhara. Its tax is counted with that of Bukhara, although it is a separate village and has a grand mosque. It was the home of many litterateurs and poets. There is a saying that in ancient times Karmina was called *Badiya-i khurdak* (the little desert). It is fourteen parasangs from Bukhara to Karmina.

Nur is a large place with a grand mosque. It has many *ribats*. Every year the people of Bukhara and other places go there on pilgrimages. The people of Bukhara take great pains in this deed. The person who goes on the pilgrimage to Nur has the same distinction as having performed the pilgrimage (to Mecca). When he returns the city is adorned with an arch because of returning from that blessed place. This Nur is called the Nur of Bukhara in other districts. Many of the followers of the Prophet are buried there. <May God be pleased with all of them till the day of judgment>.

Another village is Tawais, which is also called Arqud. In it lived people of wealth and luxury. Everyone had one or two peacocks in his home as a luxury. The Arabs had previously never seen peacocks. When they saw many peacocks there they called the village "endowed with peacocks." Its original name was forgotten, and after a time the "endowed" was also discarded, so they called it Tawais. It has a grand mosque and the (walled) town is strong. In former times there used to be a fair for ten days in the season of the month of Tir. The nature of that fair was such that all defective goods, such as curtains, covers, and other goods with defects, were sold in this fair. There was no way or means to return goods in the fair, for neither the seller nor the buyer would (return or) accept them back on any condition. Every year more than 10,000 people came to this fair, both merchants and buyers. They even came from Ferghana, Chach and other places, and returned with much profit. Because of this the people of the village became rich, and the reason for that was not agriculture. It is located on the royal road to Samarqand, seven parasangs from Bukhara.

Iskijkat has a large citadel and its inhabitants are rich. The reason for their wealth is not agriculture for the land of this village, both the wasteland and cultivated, does not equal one thousand *jufts*. Its inhabitants are all merchants. Much cloth comes from there. Every Thursday there is a market in that village. The village belongs to the ruler, Abu Ahmad al-Muwaffaq bi'llah (premier of the caliph 870–91) had given this village as a fief to Muhammad ibn Tahir, who was the amir of Khurasan, (248–259/862–873). He, in turn, sold it to Sahl ibn Ahmad al-Daghunl al-Bukhari for a price. The latter built a bathhouse there, and a large palace in a bend on the lower bank of the river. The remains of this palace existed (almost) to our time, and it was called the palace of Daghuni. Now the water of the river has destroyed that palace. The people of Iskijkat were tributary to this Sahl ibn Ahmad Daghuni, and every year they paid 10,000 *dirhams* assessment on their homes. Then they withheld the tribute from this village two or three years, turned to the ruler and requested help from him. The heirs of Sahl ibn Ahmad produced a document in the time of the amir Isma'il Samani, who saw the deed and recognized its validity. But the lawsuit dragged on a long time. Men of distinction from the city were the mediators. A settlement was made between the people of the village and the heirs of Daghuni for 170,000 *dirhams*. Thus the inhabitants redeemed the village and freed themselves from tribute, by paying the above-mentioned sum.

In this village there was no grand mosque till the time of Shams al-Mulk Nasr ibn Ibrahim Tamghaj Khan (ruled 480–72/1068–80). Among the people of the village was a man of distinction called Khwansalar. He was an important man with many followers, and was one of the tax collectors of the ruler. He built a grand mosque of great beauty at his own expense, and he spent a great sum of money on it. He performed the Friday prayer there. Ahmad ibn Muhammad ibn Nasr (Narshakhi) says that the reader of prayers in (the village of) Shargh told him that the Friday prayer was no longer performed in that mosque; (for) after a time the *imams* of Bukhara would not permit it, and they forbade the Friday prayer to be held there. The mosque remained abandoned until Qadir Khan Jibra'il ibn 'Umar ibn Tughrul Khan (492–495/1099–1102). His name was Tughrul Bek, with the "nickname" of Kular Tegin. He bought the wood of that mosque from the descendants of Khwansalar. Then he destroyed the mosque and brought its wood to Bukhara and built a religious school with the wood, near the vegetable sellers' stalls. He spent a countless sum on the work. The religious school was called the school of Kular Tekm, and the remains of this amir rest in that school.

The (village of) Shargh is opposite Iskijkat. Between them is neither garden nor vacant lot but a large river called the Samjan river. Now it is called the river of Shargh, while some call it Haramkam. A large bridge existed over the river between the two villages. In the time of Arslan Khan Muhammad ibn Sulaiman (ruled 1102–30) the bridge was built very solidly of baked bricks at his order. In the village of

Shargh there had never been a grand mosque (until) a grand mosque was built at his own expense. He (also) ordered a *ribat* built on the Iskijkat side for the needy. The village has a large citadel, which is comparable in size to the town. Muhammad ibn Ja'far (Narshakhi) mentioned that they had a market here in the olden days, where every year for ten days in the winter people came from far districts to trade and bargain. The specialties of this place were almond sweets made with grape syrup, aloe gum, wood, salted and fresh fish, and sheep and lambskins. There was much trading. In our time there is a market every Friday and merchants come from the city and surrounding districts. The specialties, which come today from this village, which the merchants bring back to their districts, are brass and cotton cloth. Muhammad ibn Ja'far said that the amir Isma'il Samani bought this village and all of its fields and estates. He gave all as an endowment for the maintenance of a *ribat*, which he built by the Samarqand gate inside the city of Bukhara. At present that *ribat* does not exist and the endowment also does not exist. Shargh and Iskijkat are the most beautiful suburbs of Bukhara; <May God the Exalted protect them>.

Zandana has a great citadel, a large market place, and a grand mosque. Every Friday the prayers are performed there, and there is trading (the same day). The specialty of the place is Zandaniji, which is a kind of cloth made in Zandana. It is fine cloth and is made in large quantities. Much of that cloth is woven in other villages of Bukhara, but it is also called Zandaniji because it first appeared in this village. That cloth is exported to all countries such as Iraq, Fars, Kirman, Hindustan and elsewhere. All of the nobles and rulers make garments of it, and they buy it at the same price as brocade.

Vardana is a large village with a large citadel and strong fortifications. It was a stronghold of kings in ancient times, but it is no longer a royal residence. It is older than the city of Bukhara. It was built by king Shapur on the frontier of Turkistan. They have a market once a week at which there is a good deal of trading. Well-made Zandaniji also comes from there.

Afshina has a large town area and a strong fort, as well as suburbs. One day a week they hold a market. The cultivated and wastelands of this village are an endowment for scholars. Qutaiba ibn Muslim built a grand mosque there and Muhammad ibn Wasi' also erected a mosque. Prayers are answered in it, and people go from the city to seek blessing there.

Barkad is an old and large village with a strong citadel. This village is called Barkad of the 'Alids because the amir Isma'il Samani bought this village and gave it as an endowment, one-third to the descendants of 'Ali and Ja'far (al-Sadiq), a third to the poor, and a third to his own heirs.

Ramitin has a large citadel and the village itself is strong. It is older than the city of Bukhara. In some books it is even mentioned as Bukhara. In ancient times it was the residence of rulers, but when the city of Bukhara was founded the rulers passed only the winters in this village. It was also thus in Islamic times. When Abu Muslim came to Bukhara he stayed in this village. Afrasiyab built it, and every time he came to this district he only stayed in this village. In the books of the Parsis it is recorded that Afrasiyab lived two thousand years, and that he was a magician. He was one of the children of king Noah. It was he who killed his son-in-law, who was called Siyavush. Siyavush had a son called Kai Khusrau who came with a large army to this country to avenge his father. Afrasiyab had made a fortress of the village of Ramitin. Kai Khusrau besieged the fortress with his army for two years, and opposite built a village, which he called Ramush because of its lovely surroundings. This village is still inhabited. He built a fire-temple in the village of Ramush, and the Magian priests say that this fire-temple is older than the fire temples of Bukhara. After two years Kai Khusrau captured Afrasiyab and killed him. The tomb of Afrasiyab is located inside a gate of Bukhara at the gate of Ma'bad on that large hill which is adjacent to the hill of Khwaja Imam Abu Hafs the great. There are special songs of the people on the killing of Siyavush. The musicians called these songs Kin-e Siyavush. Muhammad ibn Ja'far says that from his time it was three thousand years ago; <God knows best>.

Varakhsha is the largest of the villages. It used to be as large as Bukhara but older. [In some manuscripts, in place of Varakhsha, Rajfundun is written.] It was once the residence of kings. It had strong fortifications because the rulers fortified it many times. Its suburbs are similar to the suburbs of Bukhara. Varakhsha has twelve irrigation ditches and is inside the outer walls of Bukhara. There was a palace in it, the beauty of which is told in a proverb. It was built by a Bukhar Khudah more than a thousand years ago. This palace had been destroyed and abandoned for many years when Khnk Khudah restored it. It again fell into ruins, and again Bunyat ibn Tughshada, Bukhar Khudah, rebuilt it in Islamic times and made his court there until he was killed in it. Amir Isma'il Samani convoked the people of that village and said, "I shall give 20,000 *dirhams* and wood, and shall take care of the re-building of it. Part of the building is standing. You make a grand mosque out of this palace." The village people did not want it, and said that a grand mosque was unnecessary and unreasonable for their village. So the palace existed till the time of the amir Ahmad ibn Nuh ibn Nasr ibn Ahmad ibn Isma'il al-Samani. He brought the wood of that palace to the city and used it to build a mansion, which he made at the gate of the fortress of Bukhara. Every fifteen days there is a market in this village, but when the market is at the end of the year they hold it for twenty days. The twenty-first day is then New Year's day, and they call it the New Year's day of the farmers. The farmers of Bukhara reckon from that (day) and count from it. The New Year's day of the Magians is five days later.

Baikand is considered a city, and the people of Baikand do not like anyone to call Baikand a village. If a citizen of Baikand goes to Baghdad, and he is asked from whence he comes, he replies that he is from Baikand and not from Bukhara. It has a large grand mosque and prominent buildings. There were many *ribats* around the gate of Baikand until the year 240/854–5. Muhammad ibn Ja'far in his book asserted that Baikand had more than a thousand *ribats* corresponding to the number of villages of Bukhara. The reason for this is that Baikand is an exceedingly lovely place. The people of every village built a *ribat* there and settled a group. They sent them their living expenses from the village. In the winter, when the attacks of the infidels occurred, many people from every village gathered there to attack (the infidels). Every group went to its own *ribat*.

The people of Baikand were all merchants. They traded with *Chin* and the sea and became very wealthy. Qutaiba ibn Muslim had much difficulty in conquering it for it was well fortified. The (city proper) was called "the bronze city." It is older than Bukhara and every ruler who was in this district made Baikand his residence. From Farab to Baikand is a desert of twelve parasangs, and the desert is sandy. Arslan Khan Muhammad ibn Sulaiman (1102–1130) in his time ordered Baikand to be rebuilt. People assembled in it and built lovely buildings there. The khaqan (Arslan) had a mansion built for himself with great difficulty as the water of the Haramkam flows there. Contiguous to Baikand are canebrakes and large pools (all of which) is called Pargin Firakh. It is also called Qara Kul. I heard from reliable people that its size was twenty parasangs by one parasang. In the book *Masalik wa mamalik* (of Jaihani) it is stated that that place is called the Samjan Sea, where the excess water of Bukhara collects. In it are water animals, and nowhere in all of Khurasan can such a quantity of fowl and fish be found as here. Arslan Khan ordered a special canal dug to Baikand so that running water could reach the fountains of its buildings. For the water of the Haramkam sometimes flows there and sometimes not. Baikand is situated on top of a hill, but it is not high. The khaqan ordered a canal dug in this hill. The stone was found to be so hard that there were no fissures in it. During this task they were amazed for donkey-loads of grease and vinegar were expended to make the rock softer, yet they were unable to dig more than one parasang. Many people perished (there). After much energy and material had been expended it was abandoned. The story of the conquest of Baikand will be told in its place if God the Exalted permits.

Farab is counted as a city with separate suburbs. From the bank of the Oxus River to Farab is one parasang. When the water rises it comes halfway, and sometimes all the way to the city of Farab. Farab has a large grand mosque, the walls and roof of which are made of baked bricks, so there is no wood in it. There was an amir in this city who did not find it necessary to come to Bukhara for any reason. There was also a judge who gave judgments with the injustice of Shaddad. The number of villages of Bukhara is great, and we have mentioned only that group which is older and more famous than the rest.

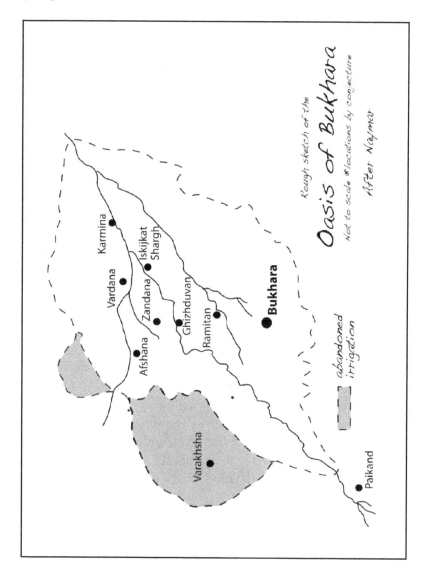

V

Account of the tiraz (textile) workshop, which was in Bukhara

In Bukhara there was a workshop between the fortifications and the town proper, near the grand mosque, in which carpets and door-hangings were woven. Yazdi cloth, cushions, prayer rugs, and hazel-colored robes for the use of the caliph were woven (all of such value) that the tax on Bukhara could be spent for one door-hanging. From Baghdad every year there came a special tax-collector, and whatever was the tax of Bukhara, he took that amount in these textiles instead. It happened that this workshop was abandoned, and the people who plied this trade dispersed. In the city of Bukhara there were artisans who were specialists in this work. Merchants came from various places and carried those cloths, just as they brought Zandaniji, to Syria, Egypt, and the cities of Rum (Byzantine Empire). They did not weave it in any other city of Khurasan. It was surprising that when some of the people of this craft went to Khurasan and manufactured the tools of this craft, and wove that material, still it did not compare in elegance and quality (to that of Bukhara). There was not a king, amir, chieftain, or functionary who did not wear clothes of this material, made in red, white, and green colors. Today Zandaniji is everywhere more famous than that material.

VI

An account of the bazar of Makh

In Bukhara there was a bazar called the bazar of [the day of] Makh. Twice a year for one day there was a fair, and every time there was this fair, idols were sold in it. Every day more than 50,000 *dirhams* were exchanged (for the idols). Muhammad ibn Ja'far has mentioned in his book that this fair existed in his time, and he was very astonished that it should be allowed. He asked the elders and shaikhs of Bukhara the reason for this. They said that the inhabitants of Bukhara in olden times had been idol-worshippers. They were permitted to have this fair, and from that time they have sold idols in it. It has remained thus till today. Abu'l-Hasan Nishapuri in his book "The Treasury of the Sciences," says that in Bukhara in ancient times was a king who was called Makh. He ordered this market to be built. He ordered carpenters and painters to prepare idols each year. On a certain day they appeared in the bazar and sold the idols, and people bought them. When their idol was lost, broken, or old, the people bought another when the day of the fair came. Then the old one was thrown away. That place, which today is the grand mosque of Makh, was a grove on the riverbank. There were many trees, and the fair was held in the shade of those trees. That king came to this fair and sat on a throne in the place which is today the mosque of Makh to encourage the people to buy idols. Everyone bought an idol for himself and brought it home. Afterwards this place became a fire-temple. On the day of the fair, when the people had gathered, all went into the fire-temple and worshipped fire. The fire-temple existed to the time of Islam when the Muslims seized power and built a mosque on that place. Today it is one of the esteemed mosques of Bukhara.

VII

Regarding the names of Bukhara

Ahmad ibn Muhammad ibn Nasr says that Bukhara has many names. In his book he calls it Numijkat. In another place I saw Bumiskat mentioned. In another place it is written in Arabic *madinat al-sufriya*, i.e.—"the copper city," and in another place, also in Arabic, *madinat al-tujjar*, i.e.—"the city of merchants." But the name Bukhara is known more than all the others. In Khurasan there is no other city with so many names. There has come down in one tradition the name Fakhira for Bukhara. Khwaja Imam, the hermit (and) preacher, related (to) Muhammad ibn 'Ali al-Nujabadi a tradition from Salman Farsi <may God be pleased with him>, who said, "The Prophet of God said that Gabriel told him that in the land of the East was a country called Khurasan. On the Judgement Day three cities of Khurasan will be adorned with red rubies and coral, and their radiance shall shine about them. Around these cities will be many angels praising, glorifying, and exalting God. They will bring forth these cities in grandeur and pomp onto the plains, as a bride who is brought into the house of her betrothed. In each of these cities will be 70,000 banners and under each banner 70,000 martyrs. In the retinue of each martyr will be 70,000 believers, speaking Persian and receiving salvation. On the Judgement Day on every side of these cities to the right and left, front and rear, for ten days of journey it will be filled with martyrs." The Prophet said, "Oh Gabriel tell me the names of these cities." Gabriel replied, "The name of one of these cities in Arabic is Qasimlya and in Persian Veshgird. The second in Arabic is Sumran, in Persian Samarqand. The third in Arabic is Fakhira, and in Persian Bukhara." The Prophet asked, "Oh Gabriel why is it called Fakhira?" He replied, "Because on the Judgement Day Bukhara shall excel all other cities in glory because of the multitude of martyrs (buried there)." The Prophet cried, "God bless (the people of) Fakhir and purify their hearts by the fear of God; improve their actions and make them among the merciful of my people." The significance of that is: from east to west it is attested that the people of Bukhara are noted for their compassion, faith, and cleanliness (of thought).

VIII

The story of the building of the citadel of Bukhara

Concerning the marvels of that (citadel), Ahmad ibn Muhammad ibn Nasr said that Abu'l-Hasan Nishapuri in the "Treasury of the Sciences" has mentioned that the reason for the building of the citadel of Bukhara was that Siyavush ibn Kaikaus fled from his father, crossed the Oxus, and came to Afrasiyab. Afrasiyab treated him kindly and gave him his daughter for a wife. Some have said he gave him all of his domain. Siyavush wanted to leave some memorial of himself in this district, which had been given in loan to him. So he built this citadel of Bukhara and usually resided there. But when he and Afrasiyab became estranged Afrasiyab killed him. He was buried in this citadel in a place (located) as you come from the Eastern gate inside the gate of the straw-sellers, which is called the gate of the Ghuriyan. The Magians of Bukhara for that reason esteemed this place. Every year before the rising of the sun, on New Year's day, every person (brings) a cock there and kills it (in memory) of him. The people of Bukhara have lamentations concerning the killing of Siyavush which are known all over. Musicians have

made songs out of them and they sing them. Singers call them
the lamentations of the Magians. This story is older than three
thousand years. So this citadel, according to tradition, was built
by him (Siyavush). Others say that Afrasiyab built it. It fell into
ruins and remained so for many years.

When Bidun Bukhar Khudah became ruler—the one whom
we have mentioned as the husband of Khatun and as father of
Tughshada—he sent a person (who) rebuilt the citadel and the
palace which had formerly existed. He wrote his name on an
iron plate and affixed it to the gate of that palace. It remained
on the door of the palace till the time of the translator (of this
book, i.e. 1128). Ahmad ibn Muhammad (ibn) Nasr (al-Qubavi)
says that when the fortress was destroyed the door was also destroyed. Ahmad ibn Muhammad ibn Nasr further mentioned
that Muhammad ibn Ja'far and Abul-Hasan Nishapuri said that
when Bidun Bukhar Khudah built this palace, it fell apart. So
he rebuilt it, and again it was destroyed. Several times he rebuilt
it but it collapsed each time. He convened the wise men and
asked their advice. They agreed that if the castle were built according to the figure of the constellation of the Great Bear in
the sky, with seven stone pillars in that form, it would not be destroyed. Another strange thing is that from the time this castle
was built, there was no ruler of it who was ever defeated in it.
He was always victorious. Another oddity is that since the time
it was built no ruler has died in it, neither pagan nor Muslim.
When the time of the death of the ruler was near, some reason
would impel him to come out of that castle and he would die in
another place. From the time of its construction to the destruc-
tion of the castle it was so.

The fortress has two gates, one the eastern, the other the
western. The eastern gate is called the gate of the Ghuriyan,
and the western gate is called the gate of the Rigistan. To the
time of the translator (of this book) it was called the gate of the
"forage sellers." A road ran from one gate to the other through
the middle of the fortress. The fortress was the place of residence of rulers, amirs, and generals. It was also a prison, and a
chancellery, while the castle was the residence of the rulers. In

olden times the harem and treasury were also in it. In the time of the translator this fortress was in ruins. Several years later Arslan Khan ordered it rebuilt and made it his residence. He made a great amir the keeper of the fortress to guard it according to instructions. This fortress had a great reputation in the eyes of the people.

When the Khwarazmshah arrived in Bukhara in the year 534/1139 or 40, the amir ZangI (ibn) 'Ali was the viceregent. He was governor of Bukhara by order of Sultan Sanjar. (The Khwarazmshah) seized him and killed him, and destroyed the fortress. It remained ruined for two years till 536/1141–2 when Alptekin became viceroy for Gur Khan. In this year he ordered the fortress rebuilt and made it his residence. The fortress was better than it had been before. In the month of Ramadan of 538 (March 1144; *sic* 548/1153) the Ghuzz army came to Bukhara. 'Ain al-Daula Qaracha Bek, and Shihab Vezir were besieged. After a struggle and great tribulation the Ghuzz army took the fortress and killed Shihab Vezir. They destroyed the fortress and it remained in ruins. When in the year 560/1164–5 they wanted to raise walls for Bukhara, baked bricks were necessary for the foundation of the wall. The foundation and the towers of (the fortress), which had been made of baked bricks, were demolished, and they used (those bricks) for the walls of Bukhara. The fortress was completely destroyed and no trace or sign of it remained. In the year 604/1207–8 the Khwarazmshah Muhammad ibn Sultan Tekesh conquered Bukhara and rebuilt the fortress. The Khitayans were vanquished, but in 616/1219–20 the Tatar army under its leader Chinghiz Khan came and fought twelve days at the gate of the fortress. They captured and destroyed it.

IX

The residences of the rulers who were in Bukhara

The area from the western gate of the fortress of Bukhara to the gate of Ma'bad is called the Rigistan. In this Rigistan were the residences of the rulers in ancient times and in the "Time of Ignorance." In the era of the Samanids, the amir Sa'id Nasr ibn Ahmad ibn Isma'il al-Samani (301–331/913–943) ordered a court erected in the Rigistan. A very fine court was built which required much expense. Near the gate of his court he ordered a building erected for the officials so that each functionary had a separate bureau in his court. At the gate of the sultan's court were the bureau of the prime minister, the bureau of the treasurer, the bureau of the chief of the guards, the bureau of the postmaster, bureau of the chief of protocol, bureau of the private lands of the ruler, bureau of the chief of (the municipal) police, bureau of religious endowments, and bureau of the judges. He ordered the bureaus erected in such an arrangement. In the time of the amir Rashid 'Abd al-Malik ibn Nuh ibn Nasr ibn Ahmad ibn Isma'il (343–350/ 954–961), his prime minister Ahmad ibn Hasan ibn al-'Utbi (*sic*), author of the book *Kitab-i*

yamini whose grave is in the quarter of the Mansur Gate in the
vicinity of the Khan's bath house, built a wonderful mosque
opposite the religious school. As a result (the beauty of) that
place was enhanced by this mosque. When the amir Rashid
fell from his horse and died, at night his slaves entered his court
and engaged in plundering. The ruler's favorites and slave girls
quarreled and the court caught fire. Everything burned including every beautiful object of gold and silver; all was destroyed
so that not a trace remained of the buildings. When the amir
Sadid Mansur ibn Nuh became king in the month of Shauwal
of the year 350 (November 961), he ordered those courts rebuilt
beside Juy-i Muliyan. Everything which had been destroyed and
lost was made better than before, and the amir Sadid (Mansur
ibn Nuh 350–366/ 961–977) lived in the court.

Now a year had not passed when, in an evening of celebration
according to ancient custom, a large fire was started. Sparks of
the fire fell on the roof of the court which again was completely
burned. The amir Sadid went in the night to Juy-i Muliyan (and
ordered the prime minister) to bring out all of the treasures and
hidden riches. He carried them out and sent them in the hands
of his confidential followers to Juy-i Muliyan. When it became
day it was found that nothing had been lost save one gold cup.
His prime minister had another one made at his own expense.
Its weight was seven hundred *mithqal* and he sent it to the treasury. From that time this place remained in ruins and it became
the Rigistan.

Another royal court in Juy-i Muliyan was a most lovely place
similar to paradise. There was no other place or residence like
Juy-i Muliyan in Bukhara because all of it was filled with courts,
gardens, parks, flower gardens, and water flowing constantly
through its lawns. The ditches intersected with one another and
flowed in a thousand directions to the lawns and flower gardens.
Everyone who viewed the flowing water wondered from whence
it came and whither it went. The artisans of the rarities of the age
and the architects have created such a marvel. A prominent person has said, "The water of life entered the park and with regret
forsook it. It uttered sighs because it had to leave this garden."

Another court extends from the gate of the Rigistan to Dash-tak, with all the houses symmetrical, wonderfully decorated in stone, with rest houses with paintings on them, four lovely gardens, beautiful fountains, and elm trees. A pavilion existed, so constructed that no ray of the sun, from the rising in the east to the setting in the west, ever fell on the pond. In these four gardens different species and kinds of fruit, such as pears, almonds, hazel-nuts, cherries, grapes, and every fruit which exists in the amber-perfumed paradise, exist also here, the best and the loveliest.

X

Juy-i Muliyan and a description of it

In ancient times the estates of Juy-i Muliyan belonged to the king, Tughshada. He gave every one of his children and sons-in-law a share. The amir Isma'il Samam bought these estates from Hasan ibn Muhammad ibn Talut, who was a general of al-Musta'in ibn al-Mu'tasim (caliph 248–251/862–865). The amir Isma'il built courts and gardens in Juy-i Muliyan, and, gave most of them as endowments to his clients, and the endowments still exist. He was always showing concern for his clients. One day the amir Isma'il was looking from the fortress of Bukhara towards Juy-i Muliyan. Sima'l-Kabir, client of his father, whom the amir very much loved and esteemed, was standing near him. The amir Isma'il said, "Will it ever be that God the Exalted will give me an opportunity to buy these estates for you? Will He give me life till I see that these estates become yours? For these estates are the most valuable, the loveliest, and with the best air, of all the estates of Bukhara." God the Exalted made it his fortune to buy all. He gave them to his clients, so that it was called Juy-i Mawaliyan, (clients) but the common people called it Juyi Muliyan.

Adjacent to the fortress of Bukhara is a plain which is called Dashtak. All of it used to be canebrake. The amir Isma'il also bought that place from Hasan ibn Muhammad ibn Talut for 10,000 *dirhams*. In the first year he received 10,000 *dirhams* from the sale of the cane. The amir Isma'il made that place an endowment for a grand mosque. After the amir Isma'il, whosoever became amir among his descendants, he built gardens and villas for himself in Juy-i Muliyan, because of its loveliness, pleasantness, and cheerfulness.

By the new gate is a place called the Karak-e 'Alawiyan (the tillage of the 'Alids). The amir Mansur ibn Nuh (961–77) built a villa there of surpassing beauty, so that a proverb was made regarding its beauty. It was built in the year 356/967. This estate of Karak-e 'Alawiyan was royal property till the time of Nasr Khan [ibn] Tamghaj Khan, (460–72/1068–80), who gave this property to scholars because it was near the city and farming would be easier for the students of religious law. In exchange he (Nasr) took land farther from the city. Juy-e Muliyan and Karak-i 'Alawiyan were occupied till the end of the rule of the Samanids when their dominion was lost and those courts went to ruin. In Bukhara there was no fixed imperial residence, but only the citadel, until the time of King Shams al-Mulk Nasr ibn Ibrahim Tamghaj Khan (1068–80) who built Shamsabad.

XI

Regarding the building
of Shamsabad

King Shams al-Mulk bought many estates at the gate of Ibrahim.
They were about half a parasang from the gate of the (public)
garden. He made gardens of surpassing beauty. He spent much
money and wealth on the buildings there and gave the area
the name "Shamsabad." Adjacent to Shamsabad he made a
meadow for the imperial horses, which he called Ghuruq. He
enclosed the place with strong walls a mile (flight of an arrow)
long. In it he built a castle and a pigeon house. In that Ghuruq
he had wild animals such as antelope, deer, foxes, and wild boar,
and all were trained (there). The walls around it were so high
that they were unable to escape. When king Shams al-Mulk
died his brother Khidr Khan (1080–1) ascended the throne. He
ordered many buildings of great beauty erected in Shamsabad.
After he also died his son Ahmad Khan (1081–9) became ruler.
He did not preserve Shamsabad so it fell into ruins.

When Malikshah came from Khurasan and arrived at
Bukhara, he caused a great deal of damage. When he came
to Samarqand he captured Ahmad Khan and brought him

to Khurasan. Then he sent him back to Transoxiana. Since
Shamsabad had been completely destroyed he ordered a court
built for himself at Juibar. He installed running water and whatever was elaborate in the garden. That court was the seat of
government of Bukhara for a period of thirty years. When
Arslan Khan became ruler (495/1102) every time he was in
Bukhara he stayed in this court. After a time he thought it wise
to order the court dismantled and carried inside the citadel. The
site remained in ruins. Several years later Arslan Khan ordered
a court built in the area of the little gate in the district of Bu
Laith. In it he ordered an imperial bath constructed. Another
bath, which had no equal, was at the gate of the court. The
court was the seat of government of Bukhara for many years.
Later he ordered the court changed into a school for students
of religious law. The bath, which was at the gate of the court,
as well as several villages were given as an endowment to that
school. He ordered a special court for himself built at the gate
of Sa'dabad.

XII

The Clan of Kashkatha

Muhammad ibn Ja'far al-Narshakhi has mentioned in his book that when Qutaiba ibn Muslim entered Bukhara and took possession of it, he ordered the people of Bukhara to give one-half of their houses and estates to the Arabs. In Bukhara there was a clan which was called the Kashkathan. They were an honored group possessing power and dignity, and they enjoyed great respect among the people of Bukhara. They were not (originally) *dihqans*, but of foreign origin. They were, however, a good family, traders, and rich. When Qutaiba solicited a division of their houses and possessions, they gave all of their houses and possessions to the Arabs and then constructed seven hundred villas outside the town. At that time the whole city was only the size, which the inner town is now. Everyone built houses for his servants and followers around his villa, and also made a garden and park at the gate of his villa. Then one moved out to the villa. They have fallen into ruins today and, for the most part, have become part of the city. Only two or three villas, called the villas of the Magians, remained in that place. Magians lived there. There were (many) fire temples of the Magians in this district, (and at the gates of the villas of the Magians) were fine and pleasant (gardens). Their estates were of great value.

Muhammad ibn Ja'far has recorded that he heard that in the reign of the amir Hamid (331–343/943–954) the estates of the villas of the Magians became expensive because the rulers of Bukhara settled there and the followers and intimates of the sovereign wished to buy the estates. So the price of one *juft* of these estates became 4,000 *dirhams*. When this information reached the amir he said that it was known to him. "Before the rulers moved to Bukhara the price of these lands was higher. If a person wanted a piece of land which a pair of oxen could work, he was unable to (find it) during the course of a year. If he were able to buy it he had to pay 12,000 *dirhams* weight of silver for every *juft*. Now the price is cheap, since every *juft* of land is 4,000 *dirhams*' weight of silver, which (means) the people have less money." Ahmad ibn Muhammad (ibn) Nasr (al-Qubavi) says that in his time the estates of the villas of the Magians were such that they were given gratis, but no one wanted them. Whatever was bought was obtained in vain because of the oppression and lack of clemency for the people.

XIII

An account of the canals of Bukhara and its surroundings

First there is the canal of Karima which is large. The second is Shapurkam, which the common folk of Bukhara call Shafurkam. It is told in a story that one of the sons of Kisra, of the house of Sasan, provoked the anger of his father and came to this district. His name was Shapur, and *pur* in the Persian language means "son." When he arrived in Bukhara the Bukhar Khudah showed him honor. Shapur liked to hunt. One day he went hunting and came to this district. At that time there was neither village there nor cultivated field but it was pasture land. The hunting area pleased him. He requested it as a fief from Bukhar Khudah in order to make it an inhabited locality. The Bukhar Khudah gave him that place. Shapur dug a great canal and gave it his name, i.e., Shapurkam. He built villages and a palace on that canal. The locality is called "the villages of Abuya." He built the village of Vardana and a castle, and made that place his residence. A great domain developed there, and at his death those villages remained with his children as an inheritance until the time Qutaiba ibn Muslim came to Bukhara.

Vardan Khudah was one of the children of Shapur, and he was a great ruler. He lived in the village of Vardana and struggled with Tughshada Bukhar Khudah. Qutaiba also fought much with him. Finally Vardan Khudah died and Qutaiba gave the kingdom of Bukhara to Tughshada. This story will be told in the account of the conquest of Baikand and Bukhara.

The third canal is called the upper Kharqana, and the fourth Kharqan *rud*. The fifth is called 'Au Khitfar, and is very large and imposing. The sixth is called Samjan, the seventh Baikan. The eighth is called upper Faravaz, and along this stream are many villages. The ninth is lower Faravaz also called Kam Daimun. The tenth is called Arvan, and the eleventh Kaifur. The twelfth is called the "river of gold," which flows into the river of the city. Every stream I have mentioned has many villages and much water. It is said that all the canals were dug by man, except the 'Au Khitfar canal, which has dug its own path without the efforts of the people of that place. Now the people of Bukhara call it the river of *nafr*.

XIV

Regarding the land tax of Bukhara and its suburbs

In the time of the Samanid dynasty and the Samani amirs it was 1,168,566 *dirhams* and five and one-half *dangs*, including the tax of Karmina. Later, everywhere the tax was lightened. Some estates were innundated by water so the government removed the tax from them. The tax was also deducted from those places, which had been ruined by water. Some (of the land) went into the hands of the 'Alids and scholars (of religious law). The government remitted the taxes from these as well. Some estates became imperial property and their taxes were erased from the registry. Such was Baikand and many other localities. The tax of Karmina was separated from that of Bukhara.

XV

The wall of Bukhara which the people call the wall of Kanpirak

Ahmad ibn Muhammad (ibn) Nasr says Muhammad ibn Ja'far al-Narshakhi did not mention this chapter in this order but mentioned some of it in the middle of his account. Abu'l-Hasan Nishapuri in "The Treasury of the Sciences," however, mentioned it in this order. When the caliphate passed to the Amir of the Faithful Mahdi, (158–169/775–785) the father of Harun al-Rashid, and none of the 'Abbasid caliphs was more pious than he, he gave the governorship of all of Khurasan to Abu'l-'Abbas al-Fadl ibn Sulaiman Tusi in the year 166/782 or 3. The latter went to Merv and resided there.

Then the chiefs, lords, and nobles of Bukhara went to him. All of the nobles of Sughd also went to Merv to hail the new governor of Khurasan. He inquired into the condition of their district. The people of Bukhara said, "We suffer from the infidel Turks who continually come without warning and plunder the villages. Now they recently came and plundered the village of Samdun and carried off Muslims into captivity." Abu'l-'Abbas Tusi said, "Is there anything you recommend I do?" Yazid ibn

Ghurak, king of Sughd, was there and said, "Long live the amir of Khurasan! In olden times, in the 'Time of Ignorance,' the Turks used to plunder the district of Sughd. A woman was ruler in Sughd. She constructed walls around Sughd and the district obtained respite from the Turks." Abu'l-'Abbas Tusi ordered Muhtadi ibn Hamad ibn 'Amr al-Dhahli, who was his amir of Bukhara, to build walls for Bukhara so that all of the villages of Bukhara would be inside those walls, similar to Samarqand, so the Turks could not enter the district of Bukhara. Muhtadi ibn Hamad ordered the wall built, and a gate constructed at every parasang, and every half-mile a strong fort. Sa'd ibn Khalaf al-Bukhari <God show him mercy>, who was a judge in Bukhara, superintended this work till the time of Muhammad ibn Yahya ibn 'Abdallah ibn Mansur ibn Haljad ibn Warraq. It was completed in the year 215/830. Every succeeding amir ordered more construction and took care of it. This represented a great trouble and expense to the people of Bukhara, for every year much money and a large labor force were necessary. So it was till the time of the amir Isma'il Samani, who freed the people of this burden. The wall fell into ruins. He said, "While I live, I am the wall of the district of Bukhara." That which he claimed he performed. He constantly fought in person and did not allow the foe victory in the province of Bukhara.

XVI

Regarding the (inner) wall of Bukhara

The people of Bukhara, through Ahmad ibn Khalid, who was the amir of Bukhara, made a request to the amir of Khurasan, Muhammad ibn 'Abdallah ibn Talha of the Tahirids (248–259/ 862–873) (*sic*), that a wall was necessary so they might lock the gates at night and remain in safety from thieves and highwaymen. So he ordered a very fine, strong wall built, and towers were erected and gates built. It was finished in 235/849 or 50. A new addition was made to this wall every time an army advanced on Bukhara. Arslan Khan, in his time, ordered another wall built in front of the old wall. Both were joined and strengthened. That one also fell into ruins. In the year 560/1165, the just and wise khaqan, support of the world and religion, Mas'ud Qilij Tamghaj Khan (566–574/1170–1178), <may God illumine his grave>, ordered a wall erected outside of the old wall of the city of Bukhara. Again it fell into ruins. In the year 560/1165 (*sic*—604/1207) the Khwarazmshah Muhammad ibn Sultan Tekesh conquered Bukhara and ordered the wall rebuilt and a rampart erected. Both were built anew. In the year 616/1219 the Tatar army came and conquered the city, and the walls again fell into ruins.

XVII

An account of the minting of dirhams and silver in Bukhara

The first person who coined silver in Bukhara was a ruler named Kana Bukhar Khudah. He ruled Bukhara thirty years. In Bukhara trading was done with cotton cloth and wheat. He was informed that in other countries silver money was coined, so he too ordered coins struck in Bukhara of pure silver, and he ordered his image with a crown be put on them. This was in the time of the caliphate of the Commander of the Faithful Abu Bakr (al)-Sadiq <God be pleased with him>. So it was till the time of Harun al-Rashid when Ghitrlf ibn 'Ata became the amir of Khurasan in the month of Ramadan of the year 185 (September 801). This Ghitrif was the brother of the mother of Harun al-Rashid. His (Harun's) mother was called Khaizuran, the daughter of 'Ata from the city of Yemen which is called Jurash. She was taken prisoner in Tabaristan and from there was brought to the caliph al-Mahdi who had two sons by her. One was Musa al-Hadi and the second was Harun al-Rashid. After Khaizuran had reached such a high position Ghitrif came to her (from Yemen) and remained with her. Harun al Rashid gave him (the governorship) of Khurasan.

At that time the coins of Khwarazm were in circulation among the people, but they took those coins with reluctance. The money of Bukhara had disappeared among the people. When Ghitrif ibn 'Ata came to Khurasan, the notables and leaders of Bukhara went to him and requested that since they had no silver left in the city, the amir of Khurasan should order money coined for them from the same die as was used for the coins of Bukhara in ancient times. "The coins should be (such) that no one would take them from us nor out of the city, so we can carry on trading among ourselves with (this) money." At that time silver was expensive. Then the people of the city were assembled and their opinion asked on this matter. They agreed that money should be struck of six things: gold, silver, brass, tin, iron, and copper. So it was done. They struck coins with the former die, with the name Ghitrif, i.e., Ghitrifi money. The common people called them Ghidrifi. The old coins had been made of pure silver, but this money, which was struck in alloy, became black, and the people of Bukhara would not accept it. The ruler became angry with them and they took the money by compulsion. The exchange was established at six Ghidrifis for one *dirham's* weight of pure silver. The government accepted it at this rate (for taxes) so that it became current. Because of this the tax of Bukhara became heavy. The tax of Bukhara in olden times was 200,000 silver *dirhams*, or a little less. After Ghidrifis were struck and became current at six for a *dirham's* weight of silver, the government compelled the people to pay (taxes) in Ghidrifis. When the Ghidrifi became dear, and it turned out that the Ghidrifi "became equivalent to the silver," the government refused to accept the silver "but demanded the Ghidrifis. The tax of Bukhara, which was something less than 200,000 silver," at once came to 1,(1)68, 567 Ghidrifi *dirhams*.

Muhammad ibn Ja'far relates that in the year two hundred and twenty (or three hundred) a hundred *dirhams* of pure silver equalled eighty-five Ghidrifi *dirhams*. Ahmad ibn Nasr (al-Qubavi) says that in the year 522/1128, when he translated this book, one hundred pure silver *dirhams* equalled seventy Ghidrifi *dirhams*. According to law (shar'ia) a *mithqal* was equal to seven and one-half Ghidrifi *dirhams*.

Muhammad ibn Ja'far stated that this Ghidrifi was coined in the castle of Makhak in the city of Bukhara. The Ghidrifi coin contains more of silver than of the other alloys. It is said that there is a grain of gold in each *dirham*, and in every ten *dirhams* (*sic*) it is found in the amount from half a *dirham's* weight to four and one-half *dang*. Many [of the copper coins called] *'adli* (and) *pishiz* were struck in Bukhara by everyone of the Samanid dynasty, and of other rulers after the Samanids. This has not been mentioned for there is nothing astonishing in that.

XVIII

The beginning of the conquest of Bukhara

Muhammad ibn Ja'far has related that when Mu'awiya sent 'Ubaidallah (ibn) Ziyad to Khurasan (governor 53–56/673–676), the latter crossed the Oxus and came to Bukhara. The ruler of Bukhara was Khatun because her son Tughshada was young. 'Ubaidallah ibn Ziyad took Baikand and Ramitin and many prisoners. He took four thousand Bukharan prisoners (as slaves) for himself. This was at the end of the year 53/673 and the beginning of the year 54/674. When he came to the city of Bukhara he drew up his ranks and arranged the war engines. Khatun sent a person to the Turks to ask their aid. She also sent a person to 'Ubaidallah (ibn) Ziyad asking for a seven days' truce. She acknowledged, "I am in your power," and sent many gifts. When help did not come in seven days she sent gifts again and asked for seven days more.

An army of Turks arrived and other (forces) assembled so the army became numerous. They fought much but finally the infidels were put to flight and the Muslims pursued them, killing many. Khatun returned to her fortress, and the troops returned to their countries. The Muslims reaped a large booty of arms, clothes, gold and silver objects. Many prisoners and the boot, with a stocking, for one of Khatun's feet, were taken. The shoe and stocking were made of gold set with jewels to the value of 200,000 *dirhams*. 'Ubaidallah (ibn) Ziyad ordered the trees up-rooted and the villages destroyed. The city was also in danger. Khatun sent a person and asked for amnesty. Peace was con-cluded for a thousand times a thousand *dirhams*, (i.e.—a million). She sent the money, which he took and departed, but he took the four thousand captives with him.

When he was removed from the governorship of Khurasan in the year 56/675 or 6, Sa'id ibn 'Uthman became the amir of Khurasan. He crossed the Oxus and came to Bukhara. Khatun sent a person to tell him, "I will make peace on the same condi-tions as I made with 'Ubaidallah (ibn) Ziyad." She sent part of the money, but suddenly the army of Sughd, Kesh, and Nakhshab arrived, and they numbered 120,000 men. Khatun regretted the peace and what she had already sent. Said said, "I feel the same." He sent the money back and declared, "There is no peace between us." Then the armies gathered, stood oppo-site each other, and arranged their ranks. God the Exalted put terror into the hearts of the infidels so that all of their forces fled without fighting. Khatun remained alone, and again she sent a person and asked for peace. She increased the tribute and sent all of it.

Sa'id said, "I am going now to Sughd and Samarqand, and you are on my road (of communications). A guarantee is neces-sary from you so that you may not cut the way and cause me trouble." Khatun gave eighty princes and *dihqans* of Bukhara as hostages to Sa'id. Sa'id went out the gate of Bukhara, departed and kept going.

A story is related that this Khatun fell in love with one of her husband's servants. People said that her son Tughshada was from this man, and that she had this son confirmed as though he were from her husband. This boy was really not the son of Bukhar Khudah. A faction of the army declared they would give this kingdom to another ruler's son who was a prince without doubt, Khatun was aware of their intention, and was considering a plan to rid herself of them when this peace was made with Sa'id. Now Sa'id wanted hostages from her. Khatun played a trick, and that group which had the intention mentioned above, she gave as hostages. So she was rid of them and Sa'id as well.

A story is told that when Sa'id made peace with Khatun he said, "You must come out and greet me." Khatun agreed, and came out to greet him. He also asked her to greet his chiefs. Khatun greeted every one of the chiefs of his army. One of the generals of the army was 'Abdallah (ibn) Khazim. He ordered a large fire kindled in his tent and he stood by it. The air became very hot. 'Abdallah was ruddy-complexioned, and his eyes also became red from the light of the fire. His head was so large that a saying was coined about it. He was terrifying and a frightening person. He was clad in armor, and drew his sword and sat down. When Khatun approached him she became afraid and quickly fled, saying,

Your beauty is adorned oh slave of God (i.e.-'Abdallah)
May the evil eye be far. What (greatness) he has made.

Story: Sulaiman Laithi has also said that when Sa'id made peace with Khatun he became sick in Bukhara. Khatun came to visit him. She had a purse full of gold. She put her hand in the purse, brought out two things and said, "This one I keep for myself; if I should become sick I eat it. The other I give to you so that you can eat it and become well." Sa'id wondered what Khatun had given with such awe and respect. When Khatun had departed Sa'id realized it was an old date. He ordered some of his followers to load five camels with fresh dates and carry them to Khatun. They brought them to Khatun. She opened the sacks and saw many dates. Then she opened her purse and brought out her date and compared it with them. They were the same as she had. She came with an apology and said, "We don't have many of these things, and I preserved these two dates for many years to be used for sickness." It is said that this Khatun was a sweet, beautiful woman, and Sa'id became enamored of her. The people of Bukhara had songs of this affair in the language of Bukhara.

It is mentioned (in tradition) that when Sa'id came to Bukhara Qutham ibn 'Abbas <may God be pleased with him>, also came to Bukhara. Sa'id honored him and said, "I shall give everyone one portion of this booty, but to you a thousand portions." Qutham replied, "I only want one part as is the decree of the religious law." After that Qutham went to Merv and died there. Some say that he died in Samarqand. <God knows best.>

When Sa'id was finished with his work at Bukhara he went to Samarqand and Sughd. He fought many battles and was victorious. At that time there was no ruler in Samarqand. He (Sa'id) brought back thirty thousand prisoners and much wealth from Samarqand. When he returned to Bukhara Khatun sent a person who said, "Since you have returned in safety return the hostages to us." Sa'id replied, "I still am not secure from you; the hostages will remain with me till I cross the Oxus." When he crossed the Oxus Khatun again sent a person. He answered, "Wait till I come to Merv." When he came to Merv he said, "Until I come to Nishapur." When he came to Nishapur he said to wait till his arrival in Kufa, and thence to Medina.

When he came to Medina he ordered slaves to take their swords and belts from them, and whatever they had of brocade garments, gold and silver. All was taken from them and rough clothes were given them in exchange. Then they were put to farming, They became very sick at heart and said, "What meanness remains which he has not inflicted upon us? He has put us in bondage and ordered us to do heavy work. If we must perish in indignity, then we should do so with one useful act." They entered the house of Sa'id, barred the doors, and killed him. Then they committed suicide.

This happened in the time when Yazid ibn Mu'awiya was caliph, and Muslim ibn Ziyad ibn Abihi became the amir of Khurasan (61–64/681–4). He came to Khurasan and prepared the army there. He arrived at Bukhara and Khatun saw the army and its array. She knew that Bukhara could not resist such an army, so she sent a person to Tarkhun, ruler of Sughd, and said, "I shall become your wife and Bukhara your city if you come and repel the Arabs from this kingdom." Tarkhun came with 120,000 men, and Bidun (*sic*) also came from Turkestan with a large army. Khatun had made peace with Muslim and had opened the gates. She had also opened the gates of the villa, which was outside the city. Bidun arrived and camped on the other side of the Kharqan stream. Muslim was informed that Bidun had arrived. Khatun swore fealty (to Bidun) and barred the gates of the city. Muslim ibn Ziyad sent a man to Muhallab and said, "Tell him to go and spy on this army, (find out) what is its strength, and whatever is in the principles of scouting, and return with it." Muhallab answered, "One does not send a man like me for this work. I am a well-known person. Send a man who, if he returns safely, will give you correct information, but if he perishes the loss will not be noticed in your army." Muslim replied, "You must go in any case." Mu-hallab replied, "If I must go, send a man with me from each banner (section) of the army, and do not inform anyone of my departure." He did so, and also sent his cousin with him. They left at night with him, and discovered (information) without the enemy army knowing it.

When it became day Muslim ibn Ziyad performed the morning prayer. He turned to the people and said, "Last night I sent Muhallab to spy." The news was spread among the army. The Arabs heard of this and said, "He has sent the amir Muhallab to obtain booty before us. If there is going to be a battle he should have sent us with him." Promptly a group mounted and went in search of Muhallab to the bank of the river. When Muhallab saw them he said, "You have made a mistake in coming. I was hidden and you are coming openly. Now the infidels will capture all of us." Muhallab counted the Muslims and there were nine hundred. He said, "By God! you should be sorry for what you have done." Then they arranged ranks. The advance guard of Bidun's army saw them. The Muslims quickly blew horns and everyone at once mounted, and they arranged their ranks.

The Turkish king attacked them and the Arabs despaired. Muhallab said, "I knew it would be thus." They asked, "What is your plan?" He said, "Advance," (but) they retreated. Bidun

overtook them and killed four hundred Muslims, and the rest
fled to their camp. The next morning Bidun crossed the river
and came near the amir of Khotan (*sic* Khurasan), until there
was only half a parasang between them. The battle was joined.
Muhallab attacked first and the battle became desperate.
The infidels attacked and surrounded him. Muhallab shouted "Help." Muslim was dismayed and said, "This is the cry of
Muhallab." 'Abdallah (ibn) Hudan was then standing in front
of Muslim, and was silent. Muslim said, "What has happened
to you that you do not speak a word?" He replied, "By God,
Muhallab would not cry for help unless he feared he would perish. I shall mount and do all I can. If it is my turn to die I
am prepared for it." At every reverse Muhallab uttered a cry.
Muslim said, "Wait for an hour." For Muslim wanted a table in
order to eat at that time. 'Abdallah (ibn) Hudan said, "Is this the
time to eat? May God satiate thee and destroy thee. Don't you
realize the situation and art thou not a man of arms?" Muslim
asked, "What is your plan now?" He replied, "Tell the cavalry
to dismount and go to the battlefield." So they did. 'Abdallah
ibn Hudan attacked and advanced towards Muhalllab, who
was surrounded and in difficulty. 'Abdallah cried, "Look behind you." When they looked they saw people coming to aid
them. They took heart, began to advance and became firm in
their task. In that interval Bidun was killed. The Muslims called
"Allahu akbar" and the infidels at once broke into flight. The
Muslims pursued the infidels and killed them till they were ut-
terly destroyed. They seized much booty and divided it on the
same day, and every horseman received 2,400 *dirhams*.

Khatun again sent a person to ask for peace. Muslim made
peace with her for a great sum. Khatun said, "I want to make a
request of you. Show me 'Abdallah (ibn) Khazim, for I once saw
his face and fainted. It seems to me he is not human." Muslim
summoned 'Abdallah (ibn) Khazim to the reception hall which
he had, and showed him to Khatun. He wore a blue silk cloak
and a red turban. When Khatun saw him she bowed to him and
sent him gifts out of admiration. Muslim, having won a victory,
collected much booty and returned to Khurasan.

XIX

An account of the governorship of Qutaiba ibn Muslim and the conquest of Bukhara

When Qutaiba ibn Muslim became the amir of Khurasan at the nomination of Hajjaj, he came and set all of Khurasan in order. He finished the conquest of Tukharistan and crossed the Oxus in the year 88/706. The inhabitants of Baikand heard of this and fortified Baikand. It was very strong. In ancient times Baikand was called the "Fortress," or "the Bronze Fortress" because of its strength.

Qutaiba fought severe battles, and for fifty days the Muslims were in sore straits and suffered hardships. They played a trick, however, and a group dug a tunnel under the walls by a tower and emerged inside the walls in a stable. They undermined the walls and made a breach. Still the Muslims could not enter the fortress and were powerless at the breach. Qutaiba announced, "To whoever enters this breach I shall give a bonus, and if he be killed I shall give it to his children." It made everyone strive to enter, and they (finally) seized the fortress. The people of

Baikand asked for quarter. Qutaiba made peace and fixed the price of tribute. He made Warqa' ibn Nasr Bahili the amir over them, while he (Qutaiba) turned towards Bukhara.

When he reached Khunbun he received news that the people of the fortress had revolted and killed the amir. Qutaiba ordered his army to go and plunder Baikand. He made their blood and property free (for the Muslims). The reason (of the uprising) was that a man in Baikand had two beautiful daughters. Warqa' ibn Nasr took possession of both. That man said, "Baikand is a large city. From all of the city why do you take my two daughters?" Warqa' did not reply, so the man sprang forward and struck him with a knife in his navel. The knife, however, did not penetrate deep and he was not killed (*sic*). When the news came to Qutaiba he returned and killed all those in the city of Baikand who were capable of fighting. He carried into captivity those who remained, so no one was left in Baikand and it was ruined.

The people of Baikand were merchants and most of them had gone on a trading expedition to *Chin* and elsewhere. When they returned they searched for their children, women, and relations, and they ransomed them from the Arabs and re-built Baikand as before. It is said there never was a city like Baikand which, having been completely destroyed and remaining empty, was then so quickly rebuilt by the hands of the same inhabitants.

Story: It is related that when Qutaiba conquered Baikand he found an idol of silver in a temple with a weight of 4,000 *dirhams*. He also found silver goblets. When he gathered together everything it amounted to 150,000 mithqals. He also found two pearls each the size of a pigeon's egg. Qutaiba asked from whence they had brought such large pearls. They said that two birds had brought them in their beaks and had placed them in the temple. Then Qutaiba gathered the elegant things and sent them, with those two pearls, to Hajjaj. He wrote a letter about the conquest of Baikand and mentioned the story of the two pearls. Hajjaj wrote an answer, "What you mentioned is known (to me), but I was astonished at the size of the pearls and about

the birds which brought them. I am even more surprised at your
liberality, that you secured such precious things and sent them
to me. May God bless you!" After this Baikand remained many
years in ruins.

When Qutaiba was finished with Baikand he went to Khunbun and fought there. He seized Khunbun, Tarab, and many
small villages. Then he went to Vardana, where there was a
ruler called Vardan Khudah. He fought many battles with him,
till finally Vardan Khudah died and Qutaiba took Vardana and
many small villages.

Among the villages of Bukhara, between Tarab, Khunbun,
and Ramitin, many troops gathered and surrounded Qutaiba.
Tarkhun, ruler of Sughd, came with many troops. Khunuk Khudah came with a large army; Vardan Khudah with his troops,
and king Kur Baghanun, nephew of the emperor of Chin also
came. He had been hired, and came with 40,000 soldiers to
give aid in the war against Qutaiba. The armies gathered and
the lot of Qutaiba grew worse. Qutaiba and his allies had (few)
arms, so he ordered that they (the soldiers) should not allow
their weapons far (from their hands), and they should not leave
(camp). As a result the price of weapons rose so high that a spear
was worth fifty *dirhams*, a shield fifty or sixty, and a coat of mail
seven hundred *dirhams*. Haiyan al-Nabatl told Qutaiba, "I myself will seek out (the enemy) so give me leave till tomorrow."
When it was morning Haiyan (al-) Nabati sent a person to the
king of Sughd saying, "I have some counsel for you. We two
should convene somewhere." Tarkhun replied, "Agreed, what
time shall we assemble?" Haiyan said, "At that time when the
army is occupied and the battle is most severe." So they did.

When the battle became fierce Haiyan (al-) Nabati saw
Tarkhun and said, "Your kingdom has slipped away from you
and you do not know it." (Tarkhun) asked, "How?" He replied,
"We can only remain here for a short time when it is warm.
Now the weather is cold and we shall have to go. While we are
here the Turks will fight against us, but when we leave they will
fight much against you, for the district of Sughd is very pleasant. There is no place in the world as pleasant as this. Do you

think they will leave Sughd to you and return to Turkistan? You will remain in difficulty, and they will take your kingdom away." Tarkhun asked, "What course should I follow?" He replied, "Make peace with Qutaiba and give him something. Inform the Turks that we have received support from Hajjaj that on the road from Kesh and Nakhshab is a mighty army. Say that you will retreat, so they will also retreat. Then make peace with us, and make a treaty with us, for we do not wish you evil or harm. Thus you can escape from this difficult situation." Tarkhun said, "You gave me good advice. I shall do this. This evening I shall retreat."

When evening came, Tarkhun sent a man to Qutaiba to make peace, and he sent gifts (worth) 2,000 *dirhams*. They blew horns and left. The *dihqans* and amirs asked what had happened. He replied, "Take care, for Hajjaj has sent a large army from the direction of Kesh and Nakhshab to attack us in the rear, so they can put us between them. I am retreating to my district." Kur Baghanun Turk sent a man and asked information about this action. He was informed and he also blew a horn and retreated. They plundered the district and left. God the Exalted removed that difficulty from the heads of the Muslims.

Qutaiba remained isolated four months, and during that time news of Qutaiba and his allies had not come to Hajjaj. He was worried about this. The Qur'an was recited and read, and prayers were offered in the mosques. Qutaiba and his allies came back to Bukhara, and this was the fourth time he had come to Bukhara. He made war, carried away wealth, and plundered part of the district. Some people were killed and others made prisoners and brought to Merv. He left and returned. <May God the Exalted protect the district of Bukhara from all misfortunes and sorrows>.

XX

The conquest of Bukhara (continued) and the establishment of Islam in it

Muhammad ibn Ja'far related that when the husband of Khatun, mother of Tughshada, died the son of the Bukhar Khudah was a small boy. Khatun held the regency. An account of that has been told in (the chapter regarding) 'Ubaidallah ibn Ziyad and Sa'id ibn 'Uthman ibn 'Affan <God be pleased with them> (Ch. XVIII). Every time a Muslim army came to Bukhara it raided in the summer and departed in the winter. Khatun fought a little with each army that came and then made peace. When her son was small everyone coveted this territory, since the Bukhar Khudah himself had seized Bukhara by force. The inhabitants of Bukhara became Muslims, but each time after the Muslims withdrew they apostatized. Qutaiba ibn Muslim converted them to Islam three times, but they (repeatedly) apostatized and became infidels. The fourth time he made war he seized the city and established Islam there after much difficulty. He instilled Islam in their hearts, and made (their religion) difficult for them in every way. They accepted Islam in appearance but in secret worshipped idols. Qutaiba thought it proper to order the people of Bukhara to give one-half of their homes to the Arabs so that the Arabs might be with them and informed of their sentiments. Then they would be obliged to be Muslims. In this manner he made Islam prevail and imposed the religious laws on them. He built mosques and eradicated traces of unbelief and the precepts of the fireworshippers. He labored a great deal and punished everyone who broke the decrees of the religious laws. He built a grand mosque, and ordered the people to perform the Friday prayer there so that God the Exalted would reward the people of Bukhara for this good (deed) on the final judgment.

XXI

On the building of the grand mosque

Qutaiba ibn Muslim built a grand mosque inside the citadel of Bukhara in the year 94/712–3. That place (formerly) had been a temple. He ordered the people of Bukhara to assemble there every Friday, for he had it proclaimed that, "Whosoever is present at the Friday prayer, I will give him two *dirhams*." The people of Bukhara, at the beginning of (their conversion to) Islam, during prayer, read the Qur'an in Persian (*sic* Sogdian), for they were unable to understand Arabic. When it was the time for the *ruku* (bowing from the waist) a man behind them shouted *bknita nkint*, and when they wanted the *sujud* (full prostration) he shouted *nkunia nkuni*.

Muhammad ibn Ja'far in his book has recorded that he saw the grand mosque of Bukhara. On its doors were images with the faces scratched out, but the rest was in its former state. He (Narshakhi) said that he asked his teacher who had first erected the doors. (His teacher) was an old man and affirmed that the reason for this was that in (olden) times it was related that outside the city were seven hundred villas where the rich people

lived and they were very arrogant. Most of them did not come
to the grand mosque. The poor wanted the two *dirhams* but the
rich had no need for them. One Friday the Muslims went to
the gates of the villas and called them to the Friday prayer and
pleaded with them. The residents, however, threw stones at
them from the roofs of the villas. They fought and the Muslims
were victorious. The latter took down the gates of the villas and
bore them away. On each gate a person had made the figure of
his idol. When the grand mosque was enlarged those gates were
used on the mosque. They erected them with the faces of the
figures erased but with the rest intact. Ahmad ibn Muhammad
ibn Nasr says that in his time one of those gates remained in
that place where you descend from the roofs to the door of the
grand mosque. If anyone wishes (to see such a door) go to the
court of the amir of Khurasan by the first door, and the second
door is what is left of those gates. The traces of the effacement
on it are still visible.

Qutaiba built that mosque which is inside the citadel.
People used to pray in it. When the Muslims increased, and
the inclination of the people for Islam grew every day, (the
worshippers) could not be contained in that mosque. (So it remained) till the time of Fadl ibn Yahya ibn Khalid Barmaki.
When he became the amir of Khurasan, (177/793 or 4) in the
time of Harun al-Rashid, the inhabitants of Bukhara gathered and decided to build a cistern (inside) the fortifications.
They also built a grand mosque between the citadel and the
city proper in the year 154/770–1. They held the Friday
prayer, however, in the (old) mosque of the fortress. When
the grand mosque became dilapidated, and the mosque of
the fortress was abandoned, the former became the bureau of
taxes. No one showed more zeal in building a large mosque
than Fadl ibn Yahya Barmaki. He spent much money (on the
grand mosque), and after that everyone added to it till the
time of the amir Isma'il Samani. The latter bought many
houses and enlarged the dimensions of the mosque by a third.
The first person who ordered lamps placed in the mosques in
the month of Ramadan was Fadl ibn Yahya Barmaki.

Story: It is related that in the time of the amir Sa'id Nasr ibn Ahmad ibn Isma'il in the month of Ramadan, on a Friday at the time when the people were in the grand mosque, the mosque suddenly collapsed. Many people were killed and there was mourning in all of the city. Some were dug out while still breathing, but in an hour they died. Some had arms or legs broken. In the entire city many people perished, so afterwards the city of Bukhara seemed empty. Soon the people of the city recovered, and all of the courtiers of the sultan gave help (to rebuild). Abu'l-Qadi was in charge of that work. The mosque was finished in one year.

Yet another time, after a year, it was destroyed again. Both sides of the *qibla* fell down, but there were no people in it. It was rebuilt in the course of five years, and Abu 'Abdallah al-Jaihani built the minaret completely at his own expense in the year 306/918. He was the prime minister of the sultan at that time. This grand mosque was adjacent to the citadel. It existed till the end of the rule of Ibrahim Tamghaj Khan (433–460/1041–1068). Tamghaj Khan had another son Shams al-Mulk Nasr ibn Ibrahim (460–473/1068–1080), who advanced on Bukhara. Saifas strengthened the citadel of Bukhara. Shams al-Mulk engaged in battle at the gate of the citadel of Bukhara. From the minaret of the grand mosque they shot arrows into the citadel. As a result the people in the citadel were in sore straits. Shams al-Mulk (*sic* Saifas?) ordered fire (arrows) shot from the fortifications. The top of the minaret was made of wood and caught fire. Firebrands fell down on the grand mosque and it also burned.

After king Shams al-Mulk had seized the citadel, and the kingdom of Bukhara surrendered to him, he ordered the grand mosque rebuilt. He also ordered a trench dug between the citadel and the grand mosque. The top of the mosque was built of baked bricks. The maqsura (ante-chamber) and the court where the maqsura was located, he ordered built farther from the citadel. The nobles and rich all gave help to finish this structure. The burning of the mosque was in the year 460/1068, and in 461/1069 it was rebuilt.

Muhammad ibn Abu Bakr (Narshakhi) says he heard from trustworthy friends that the maqsura, minbar, and mihrab which are in (the mosque in) Bukhara, were ordered by king Shams al-Mulk. They were carved and decorated in Samarqand and brought to Bukhara. The mosque remained in this state till the time of Arslan Khan Muhammad ibn Sulaiman (495–524/1102–1130), who ordered the grand mosque placed even farther from the citadel, so damage would not happen to it as (had occurred) in the time of Shams al-Mulk. Arslan Khan bought many houses in the city proper, and that part of the grand mosque nearest the citadel he ordered removed. The minaret near the citadel he ordered excavated and transferred into the city. There was nothing similar to it anywhere in exquisite craftsmanship and beauty. When it was finished and the top put on it, a little remained before it was completed. But it was bewitched and the minaret fell down and struck the grand mosque, one-third of which was destroyed. The painted, carved wood all broke. Again Arslan Khan ordered the minaret erected. They took pains to make it durable, so its top was made of baked bricks. All was done at his personal expense. The grand mosque which he ordered was (built) in 515/1121.

Of the total of mosques there are five with courtyards. The two in the city proper, with the minarets, are the work of Shams al-Mulk. The large courtyard and the *maqsura* are also the work of Shams al-Mulk. Between them are two courtyards (dating) from ancient times. The one (mosque) near the citadel remains from Isma'il Samani, built in the year 290/902. The other, near the court of the amir of Khurasan, is the work of the amir Hamid Nuh ibn Nasr (ibn Ahmad) ibn Isma'il Samani, built in the year 340/951 of the Hijra of the Prophet <may God bless and preserve him>.

XXII

An account of the place of prayer for festivals

When Qutaiba ibn Muslim built the grand mosque it was inside the citadel. Inside the city, in a place called the Rigistan, he made a place for the holiday prayer, to which he brought out the Muslims to perform the prayers for festivals. He ordered the people to bring their arms with them because Islam was still new, and the Muslims were not safe from the infidels. Today the custom remains that all those who have weapons take them out with them. The gate (facing the area) is called the gate of the court of Ma'bad. This Ma'bad al-Halil was (formerly) the amir of Bukhara. In this place of worship the festival prayers were performed for many years.

(All) could not be contained (in it), so the amir Sadid, Mansur ibn Nuh ibn Nasr (961–77), bought enclosures and lovely gardens on the Samatin road for a high price, and he spent much money on them. He made it a place for the holiday prayers, and ordered a fine *minbar* and *mihrab* (erected). He also ordered columns erected so that the elders might call the prayer from them so people could hear. From this place of prayer to the gate of the citadel of Bukhara was half a parasang. It was all full of people (at prayer-time), and for many years the holiday prayers were held here. This began in the year 360/970–1. It was the place of worship till the time of Arslan Khan. He ordered the place of worship (for festivals) built near the city so it wouldn't be so difficult for the people, and if foes attacked the city the people would not be absent. At the gate of Ibrahim was a garden fit for kings, which was called Shamsabad. The garden had been destroyed and farming was practiced in it. The Turkish khaqan ordered all of it enclosed and built high walls around it. The *minbar* and *mihrob* were made of baked bricks, and in it were columns for the elders (reciters of prayers). That was in the year 513/1119 from the flight of the Prophet. <May God bless and protect him and his family>.

XXIII

On the division of the city of Bukhara between the Arabs and the natives

Muhammad ibn Ja'far relates from Hatim the Jurist, that when Qutaiba came to Bukhara the fourth time and seized the city, he made peace on condition that every year 200,000 *dirhams* be sent to the caliph, and 10,000 to the amir of Khurasan. They had to give half of their houses and fields to the Muslims, and fodder for the horses of the Arabs, firewood, and whatever was levied in taxes. People who were outside the city also had to give. In the city were villas, and some quarters were dispersed far from one another, like villages. The city proper had seven gates. The first was called the gate of the bazar, because in that time there was no bazar by any other gate of the city except here. We call it the "gate of the spice sellers."

Then Qutaiba divided the city so that the part from where you come in by the gate of the "spice-sellers" to the gate of the citadel and from there to the gate of Nun was given to (the tribes of) Rabi'a and Mudar, and the remainder to the Yemenites.

When you enter the city proper the first quarter to the left is called the "quarter of the rogues." Before this time a Christian church was there, but now it is a mosque called the mosque of the Bani Hanzala. When you come into the city, to the right is a section called the district of Wazir ibn Aiyub ibn Hassan.

It is also called the "district of the castle." This Wazir ibn Aiyub was one of the captains of Qutaiba, and his father had been the amir of Bukhara. He was the first person in the time of Islam who was appointed the amir in Bukhara by Qutaiba ibn Muslim. The successive amirs of Bukhara lived in this "district of the castle." There was a separate court there for each of the amirs of Bukhara.

There was a *dihqan* called Khina who changed his name to Ahmad when Islam was brought there. All of this "district of the castle" belonged to him. There was a castle in this quarter where the *dihqans* and the amirs of Bukhara used to live. Afterwards the castle passed from the rightful owner. In 150/767 the descendants of this *dihqan*, Kadra-e Khina by name, made a plea before Abu Ja'far Dawaniqi (Mansur), who was caliph, for this castle, and they presented a deed. The first boundary (according to) it was the walls of the city adjoining the site of the "green grocers stalls." The second boundary was also along the city walls adjacent to the bazar of the "pistachio shellers." The third boundary was a straight road which led from the gate of Nun to the middle of the city. From the gate of the 'spice sellers' to the gate of Nun is all one area, which is one-fourth of the city proper. It was included in this deed. (In addition there were) one thousand shops in the city of Bukhara, and seventy-five private villages on the river of Bukhara and on the Upper Faravaz, which existed in Islamic times. They presented claim to all of this before the caliph. They offered documents and witnesses gave proofs. The caliph ordered it registered and (the decision) brought to Bukhara. Everything was returned to them. Afterwards their children little by little sold it to everyone till it was dispersed among the people.

Entering by the gate of the "spice sellers," you come to the gate of the Bani Sa'd and the mosque of the Bani Sa'd. Hasan

ibn 'Ala' Sa'di, who was a great man, had a villa of such a high
value inside the city proper that there was no king who had a
similar one. He built up the district of 'Ala' to the gate of 'Ala',
and he built this enclosure. Every month he obtained 1,200 *dinars*
from the produce of this area. He also owned estates in the city.

Story: Hasan ibn Tahir, who was the amir of Khurasan
(*sic*, 'Abdallah ibn Tahir ibn al-Husain 213–230/828–44),
had a chief minister who was called Hafs ibn Hashim. The
latter wished to buy these lands from them (the owners), but
they would not sell. Because of that he imprisoned them and
inflicted much torture on them. Once a week he called them to
him and sought to buy the estates. When they would not sell he
sent them back to the prison and ordered the punishment increased. In such a state fifteen years passed. They endured the
punishment and pain, but they did not sell their possessions.
One day Hafs ibn Hashim called them and said, "You have endured punishment for a long time. What do you think will finally
happen to you?" Hasan ibn 'Ala' said, "One of three things will
happen. Either you will die, your master will die, or we shall
die." On the same day Hafs ordered an increase in their torture
and punishment. A month had not passed from the time of this
conversation when the amir of Khurasan died. They raised a
revolt and destroyed the prison. Hafs ibn Hashim fled and they
plundered his court. Hafs remained concealed till he died, and
Hasan ibn 'Ala' returned to Bukhara with his brothers.

When you pass from the gate of the Bani Sa'd there is the
gate of the Bani Asad. In the "Time of Ignorance" this gate
was called the gate of Muhra. When you come out and descend
from that gate, there is the court of the amir of Khurasan. The
other gate is called the "gate of the citadel," because if you go
out from this gate the fortifications are in front of you. Today
that quarter is in ruins, namely the quarter called Faghsadra,
and now it is a burial ground. The houses of the Arabs were
mainly by that gate. That gate is the strongest of all and has a
large arch, the length of which is sixty paces. Under the arch are
many houses. An amir called Subash Tekm built this structure.
His mausoleum is also in this place.

The next gate is the gate of Haqrah. Khwaja Imam Abu Hafs the great, Bukhari, lived in that quarter. He went from Bukhara to Baghdad and became a student of Imam Muhammad Husain Shaibani <God bless him>. There was no other person like him in the district. He was one of the honored teachers of Bukhara. He was an ascetic as well as a man of knowledge. Because of him Bukhara became the "Dome of Islam." That was because the people of Bukhara were educated; knowledge was diffused there, and the imams and wise men were honored. He was the cause of it. His son Abu 'Abdallah also attained such a high degree of knowledge that when a caravan returned from the pilgrimage, their scholars came to Khwaja Imam Abu Hafs and asked him questions. He said, "You come from 'Iraq; why did you not ask the learned men of Iraq?" One replied, "I disputed the question with the learned men of 'Iraq, and they were unable to give me an answer. They told me when I come to Bukhara to ask Khwaja Imam Abu Hafs Bukhari about this matter, or his children." Then he gave a proper answer to the question. Every night and day Khwaja Abu Hafs twice read the Qur'an through, and still (had time) to teach the people. When he became old and weak he read the Qur'an through only once. When he became more feeble he read only half the Qur'an until he died. <May God forgive him, with mercy and blessing.>

A story (is) told that Yahya ibn Nasr said, "I was with Khwaja Abu Hafs when the morning prayer was finished. He sat with his face towards the *qibla* and was reading something when the sun rose. Then he saw that the people were not present at his lecture on religious knowledge. He rose and made four *ruku'* in prayer and read the *suras,* "the Cow," "the Family of 'Imran," "The Women," and "the Table," during the four *ruku'* When he gave the blessing the people were still not present. He rose and performed twelve *ruku'* of prayer, reading to the *sura* of "Thunder."

Muhammad ibn Talut Hamadani narrated from the (book) *Fasl al-khitab* that in Bukhara there was an amir called Muhammad Talut. One day he said to Khishwiya, who was his prime minister, "We must go on a visit to Khwaja Imam Abu Hafs and

find him." This Khishwiya was one of the influential and powerful men of Bukhara. He said, "You should not go to him for when
you are with him you will be unable to speak to him before his
face because of awe for him." He replied, "I shall go in any case."
So he went with his prime minister to Khwaja Imam Abu Hafs.
The latter was in the mosque praying. After the mid-day prayer,
when he had given the blessing, the prime minister entered and
said, "The amir has come. Has he permission to enter?" (The
Khwaja) replied, "He has," and turned his face to the *qibla*. The
amir entered, greeted him and sat down. He was unable to say a
single word. The Khwaja, <may God show him mercy>, asked,
"What need do you have?" Every time he tried to say a word he
was unable to speak. When the amir met Khishwiya, the latter
asked, "What (impression) did you obtain of Khwaja Abu Hafs?"
The amir replied, "It was just as you said; I remained in awe.
Several times I went to the caliph and spoke with him. At those
discourses I was not in awe of the caliph. Here I was unable to
speak out of respect for him (Abu Hafs)."

It is related from Muhammad ibn Salam Baikandi, who was
an ascetic and scholar, that in a dream he had seen the Prophet
<may God give him mercy and peace>, in Bukhara, in the
bazar of Kharqan. The area from the beginning of the quarter of the Magians to the section of the *dihqans*, was called the
bazar of Kharqan in olden times. He said he saw the Prophet
sitting on that same camel, which is mentioned in tradition,
with a white cap on his head. A large crowd was standing
before him showing delight at the coming of the Prophet.
They said, "Where will we lodge the Prophet <may God bless
him>?" Then they lodged him in the house of Khwaja Imam
Abu Hafs. (He said) he saw the Khwaja Abu Hafs sitting before the Prophet and reading "The Book." For three days the
Prophet remained in the house of Abu Hafs, while he read
"The Book" and the Prophet listened. In those three days he
never once corrected him, for all was correct. Today the home
of the Khwaja does not exist, although several times people rebuilt it; but traces of it still remain. His prayer-cell also remains
in that house, and prayers are answered there.

He died in 217/832 and his ashes are by the new gate which is well known. It is a place where prayers are answered. The mound is called the hill of Khwaja Imam Abu Hafs. There are mosques and monastery-cells there. Adjoining it live wild animals. The people consider that earth blessed, and they call that place the gate of Haqrah (Road of Truth) for it was there that people brought a fatwa (judicial decision) to Khwaja Abu Hafs and he interpreted it correctly. So it is rightly called Haqrah.

The seventh gate was called the new gate because it was the last gate of the city proper. If you enter this gate on the right hand is the mosque of the Quraish, which is near the home of Khwaja Abu Hafs. They called this the mosque of the Quraish because Muqatil ibn Sulaiman al-Quraishi lived there. This Muqatil was the master of Haiyan who was the client of Talha ibn Hubaira al-Shaibam. This Haiyan was an influential and prominent man in Khurasan. He made peace between Qutaiba and Tarkhun, the king of Sughd, at the time when the infidels had surrounded the former at the gate of Bukhara. This same Haiyan installed an army in Ferghana which (later) killed Qutaiba. A pond of Haiyan is named after him. The grave (lit. ashes) of Qutaiba in Ferghana is well-known. He rests in the vicinity of the *ribat* of the general, in the village called Kakh. From nearby districts people make pilgrimages to it. Qutaiba was fifty-five years old when he became a martyr. <May God be pleased with him>.

XXIV

An account of the house of Saman and their lineage

When Asad ibn 'Abdallah al-Qushairi (*sic*, al-Qasri) became the amir of Khurasan he came and remained there until he died in the year 166/782–3 (*sic*, 120/738). It is said that he was a man of good works and generous. He was so thoughtful that he took care of the great and old families (of Khurasan). He held in esteem the people of noble origin both of the Arabs and the natives. When Saman Khudah, who was the ancestor (of the Samanids), fled from Balkh and came to him in Merv, the amir showed him honor and respect. He (the amir) subdued his foes and gave Balkh back to him. Saman Khudah accepted Islam from him. He was called Saman Khudah because he had built a village which was called Saman. They called him by that name, just as the amir of Bukhara (was called) Bukhar Khudah. When a son was born to Saman Khudah, out of friendship for the (governor), he named him Asad. This Asad was the grandfather of the late amir Isma'il Samani, that is Isma'il (ibn Ahmad) ibn Asad ibn Saman Khudah. Saman Khudah was one of the children of King Bahrain

Chubin. From the time (of Asad) the power of the Samanids increased every day till it attained what it did.

Ahmad ibn Muhammad ibn Nasr says Muhammad ibn Ja'far has related a story in his book from Muhammad ibn Salih al-Laithi and Abul-Hasan Maidani that in the time of Asad ibn 'Abdallah al-Qushairi a man appeared and exhorted the people of Bukhara to accept Islam. Most of the people of Bukhara were *dhimmis* who paid the poll tax. A group accepted (his exhortations) and became Muslims. The ruler of Bukhara was then Tughshada. He became angry, for he was really an unbeliever at heart. He wrote a note to the amir of Khurasan, Asad ibn 'Abdallah, that in Bukhara a man had appeared who was causing unrest in the province. "He has incited a group to oppose the ruler. They say they have accepted Islam, but they lie. They proclaim it in speech, but in their hearts they are concerned with their old belief. This is all to cause unrest in the province and in the kingdom, and to avoid paying the tax." Because of this Asad ibn 'Abdallah wrote to his tax collector, Sharik ibn Harith and ordered him to seize that group and surrender them to the ruler of Bukhara, to dispose of them as he wished.

It is related that this group was in a mosque, all speaking loud voices, "I testify there is no God but Allah, and I testify that Muhammad is His servant and messenger." They cried, "Oh Muhammad, Oh Ahmad!" (but) the Bukhar Khudah Tughshada cut off their heads. No one had a chance to plead for mercy. So four hundred people were decapitated and (their heads) placed on gibbets, and the rest were made prisoners in the name of Asad ibn 'Abdallah and sent to him in Khurasan. Not one of this group apostatized, and every one who remained alive remained a Muslim. Asad ibn 'Abdallah did not keep them from Islam. When Tughshada Bukhar Khudah died, that group returned to Bukhara <God knows best>.

XXV

The story of Nasr (ibn) Saiyar and the killing of Tughshada

In the year 166/782 (*sic*, 120/738) Asad ibn 'Abdallah died and Hisham ibn 'Abd al-Malik ibn Marwan (105–125/723–743) made Nasr (ibn) Saiyar the amir of Khurasan, (120–130/ 738–748) and sent him the investiture for Khurasan. When he came to Transoxiana he made raids on the Turks. He conquered Ferghana and scattered them (the Turks). Then he returned to Samarqand. When he arrived in Samarqand Tughshada Bukhar Khudah went to him. Nasr showed him honor and held him in respect, for Nasr had requested his daughter (in marriage). Tughshada had given him the upper estates of Khunbun which were called the "tillage of the 'Alids."

When Tughshada came to Nasr (ibn) Saiyar, the latter was sitting at the gate of his court. It was the month of Ramadan at the time of the setting of the sun. Nasr (ibn) Saiyar was speaking with Tughshada Bukhar Khudah when two *dihqans* from Bukhara entered. Both were relatives of Bukhar Khudah and both had accepted Islam from Nasr ibn Saiyar. They were nobles. They complained of the tyranny of Bukhar Khudah before Nasr (ibn) Saiyar and claimed that he had seized their villages. The amir

of Bukhara, Wasil ibn 'Amr, was also there, and they (also) asked
redress from him. They remarked, "These two act as one and
confiscate the properties of people." Tughshada whispered soft-
ly to Nasr (ibn) Saiyar, and they suspected that Tughshada had
requested Nasr (ibn) Saiyar to kill them. They came to an agreement and said to each another, "Since Bukhar Khudah wishes to
kill us let us for once follow our hearts' desire." Tughshada said
to Nasr (ibn) Saiyar, "Since both of them accepted the faith from
you, why then, oh amir, are there daggers on their belts?" Nasr
(ibn) Saiyar asked them, "Why do you carry these daggers at your
belts?" They replied, "There is enmity between us and Bukhar
Khudah, and we do not consider ourselves safe from him." Nasr
(ibn) Saiyar ordered Harun ibn Siyavush to take their daggers
from their belts, and the amir turned an angry glance at them.
The two *dihqans* drew farther away and planned to kill them.

Nasr (ibn) Saiyar rose for the prayer. He pronounced the for-
mula and led the prayer. Bukhar Khudah sat on a throne and
did not pray, for he was still an unbeliever in secret. When Nasr
(ibn) Saiyar finished the prayer he entered the curtained court
and called Tughshada. Tughshada stumbled at the door of the
court and fell. One of the two *dihqans* ran (to him) and struck
Bukhar Khudah with a knife in his stomach and pierced it. The
other one came to Wasil, who was still praying, and stabbed him
with a dagger in the stomach. When Wasil saw him, he quickly
drew his sword and cut off the head of that *dihqan*, and both
died at the same time. Nasr (ibn) Saiyar ordered the *dihqan* who
had stabbed Bukhar Khudah to be put to death. Then Bukhar
Khudah was carried into the curtained court and Nasr (ibn)
Saiyar had him placed on his own bed. He made him comfort-
able and called a competent doctor, and ordered him to treat
him. Bukhar Khudah made a will and died in an hour. His servants entered and removed his flesh and brought his bones to
Bukhara. He had been ruler for thirty-two years. Nasr (ibn)
Saiyar recited a prayer for Wasil (ibn) 'Amr and buried him inside his own curtained court. He confirmed Bishr (*sic* Qutaiba)
ibn Tughshada as Bukhar Khudah, and Khalid ibn Junaid became the amir of Bukhara <God knows best>.

XXVI

The story of Sharik ibn Shaikh al-Mahri

There was an Arab who lived in Bukhara and he was a brave man. He held the Shia' faith and urged the people to support the children of the Amir of the Faithful 'Ali <may God be pleased with him>, for the caliphate. He said, "We are now free from the affliction of the Marwanids. The plague of the house of 'Abbas is not necessary for us. The children of the Prophet must be the successors of the Prophet." Many people came to support him. The amir of Bukhara was 'Abd al-Jabbar ibn Shu'aib, and he gave him his loyalty. The amir of Khwarazm 'Abd al-Malik ibn Harthama also pledged him allegiance, and they formed a league. The amir of Brzm(?), Mukhallad ibn Husain, professed loyalty to him and joined him. They agreed to spread this doctrine and to fight anyone who opposed it.

This news came to Abu Muslim, and he sent Ziyad ibn Salih to Bukhara with ten thousand men. He ordered him, "When you come to Amui halt and send out scouts to give you information on the situation of the outlaw Sharik. Then go to Bukhara with caution." Abu Muslim departed from Merv and made camp at Kushmihan a journey of one stage from the Amui road. He gathered his army from all sides. He told Ziyad ibn Salih, "I shall remain here. If you need troops send me a message and I shall send them."

Ziyad came to Bukhara and made his camp. Sharik ibn Shaikh, with a large army, made camp at the gate of Bukhara. Most of the people of Bukhara joined him to fight Ziyad ibn Salih and Abu Muslim. They fought for thirty-seven days, and there was no day that victory was not on the side of Sharik. Every day many soldiers of Ziyad ibn Salih were killed or taken prisoner.

Sulaiman Quraishi, patron of Haiyan (al-) Nabati went with five hundred men up to the gate of the city. Hamza al-Hamdani came out of the city of Bukhara against him. Sulaiman had placed four hundred men in an ambush, and came with one hundred men to fight Hamza al-Hamdani. Hamza thought that his force was no larger, and advanced and fought him. Then the four hundred men came out of the ambush and killed a great number of people. The rest fled into the city. Qutaiba ibn Tughshada Bukhar Khudah came with 10,000 men. He raised the army (*sic:* black) banner and entered battle on the side of Ziyad ibn Salih He ordered the gates of the castles opened, and there were seven hundred castles at the gates of Bukhara. He ordered the people of the castles to raise the army (*sic*: black) standard. There were more inhabitants in these castles than in the city itself, but in the city there were (Arabs) among the townspeople. There was not one Arab in the castles. Bukhar Khudah ordered the people of the villages and the castles to lock their gates to the army of Sharik, and not to give them food or fodder. He ordered food and fodder brought to the camp of Ziyad.

The army of Sharik had all kinds of difficulty and was in sore straits. There was starvation and their animals did not receive fodder, so they were useless for action. They finally agreed on a plan to go nearer the gate of the city so they could bring food and fodder from the city. They could stand with their backs to the city and their faces towards the enemy, and another army from the city could aid them. However they could not go in day

time because the camp of Ziyad and Bukhar Khudah blocked
the road. They advanced at night until they came one parasang
from the city. Ziyad received news of it. He moved forward,
blocked the road, and engaged in combat. It was severe and
the army of Ziyad and Bukhar Khudah was defeated. Bukhar
Khudah said, "It is best if we attack their rear guard, for if we
advance ahead of them they will seize our place and we shall be
in danger. When we attack their rear guard their advance guard
will rush towards the city, but they will quickly turn to engage in
battle, then we will prevail."

So they did, and they waited till some of them had gone.
Then they fell on the rear guard and engaged in battle. The
(enemy) fled and arrived at Naukanda. Bukhar Khudah said to
Ziyad ibn Salih, "This group is hungry, and they have neither
seen nor eaten grapes or melons this year. When they arrive at
Naukanda let us wait until they are occupied with (eating) grapes
and melons, and fruit, and their advance guard has reached the
city. Then we shall fall on them." When they (Sharik's army)
reached Naukanda they separated in search of grapes, melons, and fruit. The advance guard had arrived at the city when
Bukhar Khudah and Ziyad attacked the (rest). They killed a
great number of people, and the rest were put to flight.

Meanwhile, Sharik ibn Shaikh, who was the leader of those
people, fell from his horse and was killed. Ziyad ibn Salih
dismounted at the gate of Makh, now called the mosque of
Maghak, on the bank of a canal. He ordered the city set on fire.
The city burned three days and nights. He ordered a proclamation that everyone who came out to him would receive amnesty.
Ziyad stationed the army farther from the city so they could
come out. A son of Sharik and one of the captains of his army
arrived at the gate of the city in the night. Both were seized and
brought to Ziyad. He ordered them hanged. The people of the
city still remained hostile, and no one came out on this proclamation. After three days Ziyad approached the gate of the city.
He stayed in the castle of Bukhar Khudah, which was by the
gate of the fortress in the Rigistan. He ordered the army to go
to the city gate and begin the battle. They fought and shouted

Allahu akbar so the earth trembled. The battle was fierce. Some prominent people came out of the city and fought at the gate of "the spice sellers." Many people of the city were killed. Ziyad ordered anyone from the city who was captured to be hanged on the city gate. Finally the city was taken. When Ziyad had finished with Bukhara he went to Samarqand. He fought there and then returned to Khurasan <God knows best>.

XXVII

An account of the appearance of Muqanna' and his followers of the "White Raiments"

Ahmad ibn Muhammad ibn Nasr says that Muhammad ibn Ja'far (Narshakhi) has included this chapter in his book, but it is incomplete. Ibrahim, who is the author of the "Account of Muqanna'," and Muhammad ibn Jarir al-Tabari say that Muqanna' was a villager from the vicinity of Merv, from a village called Kaza. His name was Hashim ibn Hakim. At first he was a bleacher, but afterwards he busied himself studying science. He acquired knowledge of every sort; he studied conjuring, the art of incantations, and talismans. He knew conjuring very well, and also pretended to prophecy. Mahdi ibn Mansur killed him in the year 167/783. He learned incantations and was extremely clever. He had read many books of the science of the ancients and was a master in necromancy. His father was called Hakim and he had been one of the captains of the amir of Khurasan in the days of Abu Ja'far Dawaniqi (Mansur). He was from Balkh, and he was called Muqanna' because he kept his head and face covered. (This was) because he was exceedingly ugly; his head was bald, and he was blind in one eye. So he constantly wore a piece of green cloth over his head and face.

Muqanna' had been one of the captains of Khurasan in the time of Abu Muslim, leader of the 'Abbasid revolt. Then he became the chief minister of 'Abd al-Jabbar Azdi. He made a claim to prophecy, and this lasted for some time. So Abu Ja'far Dawaniqi sent a man to him, brought him from Merv to Baghdad and imprisoned him. After some years, when he had secured freedom, he returned to Merv. He gathered people around him, saying, "Do you know who I am? The people replied, "You are Hashim ibn Hakim." He said, "You are wrong. I am your lord and lord of all the world." <May ashes be in his mouth.> He continued, "I call myself by whatever name I wish. I am the one who showed myself to people as Adam, then in the form of Noah, also in the form of Abraham, Moses, then in the guise of Jesus, Muhammad the Prophet, in the guise of Abu Muslim, and now in this guise which you see." The people said, "Others considered themselves prophets, but you pretend to be God." He replied, "They were corporeal. I am the soul which was in them. I have the power to be in any guise I wish to show."

He wrote letters to every district and gave them to his missionaries. In these letters he wrote thus, "In the name of God the merciful and compassionate, From Hashim ibn Hakim, lord of lords, to so-and-so son of such a one. Praise be to God, there is no other God than He, God of Adam, Noah, Abraham, Jesus, Moses, Muhammad, and Abu Muslim. Verily al-Muqanna' has strength, power, glory, and proof. Accept me and realize that I have dominion. <Curse him.> Glory and omnipotence are mine. There is no other God but me.<May ashes be in his mouth.> He who follows me will go to paradise, but he who does not accept me will rest in hell."

At that time he was in Merv but his missionaries went everywhere, and he turned many people from the (true) path. In Merv there was an Arab called 'Abdallah ibn Amr, who joined Muqanna' and gave him his daughter for a wife. This 'Abdallah crossed the Oxus and came to Nakhshab and Kesh. Everywhere he induced people to follow Muqanna' <Curse him>. He turned many people from the road (of truth). In Kesh and its suburbs they were (especially) numerous. The first village which joined Muqanna' and proclaimed his faith was a village of Kesh called Subakh. Their leader was 'Umar Subakhl and they raised a revolt. Their amir was a pious Arab and they killed him. In Sughd most of the villages accepted the faith of Muqanna'. Many of the villages of Bukhara turned to infidelity and made manifest their infidelity. This evil increased and the afflictions on the Muslims became severe. They (the infidels) attacked caravans, pillaged villages, and caused much devastation.

The reason of the departure of Muqanna' for Transoxiana was this: when the news of Muqanna' was spread in Khurasai Humaid ibn Qahtaba, the governor of Khurasan, ordered him imprisoned. He fled from his village and remained hidden. It became known to him that a large number of people had joined his faith in Transoxiana and were publicly professing his faith. He resolved to cross the Oxus river. The amir of Khurasan had ordered guards to watch for him on the bank of Oxus. A hundred horsemen constantly passed up and down river, so if he tried to cross they would seize him. He camie to the bank of the Oxus with thirty-six followers, made a raft and crossed the river. He went to the district of Kesh, which submitted to him and the people esteemed him. On the mountain Sam was a very strong fortress. In it were running water; trees, and cultivated fields. There was another fortress, stronger than this one, which he ordered rebuilt. There he collectcd much wealth and innumerable possessions, and posted guards.

The people of the "White Raiments" became numerous and the Muslims were impotent before them. A group (of fugitives) came to Baghdad while Mahdi was caliph. He became grieved and sent many troops to fight him (Muqanna'). Finally he himself came to Nishapur to put down that uprising. He feared that there was a danger that Islam would be lost and the religion of Muqanna' would spread throughout the entire world. Muqanna' invited the Turks and permitted them (to take) the life and possessions of the Muslims. Many troops came from Turkistan in the hope of plunder. They pillaged the districts and carried the women and children of Muslims into captivity, and killed (others).

When first they appeared before Bukhara, a group of the "White Raiments," who were followers of Muqanna', went to the village called Numijkat. At night they entered the mosque and killed the muezzin and fifteen people. Then they killed all of the people of the village. This was in the year 159/775–6, while the amir of Bukhara was Husain ibn Mu'adh. There was a man of Bukhara who was one of the leaders of the followers of Muqanna'. He was called Hakim (ibn) Ahmad, and with him were three other captains. One was named Khishwi, the second Baghi, both from the castle of Fudail, and the third was callled Kirdik from the village Ghijduvan. These three men were fighters, vagrants, ferocious and thieves.

After they killed the people of the village and news of this came to the city, the people of Bukhara assembled and went to the amir. They said, "We must fight these people in "White Raiments" with all possible means." Husain ibn Mu'adh with his troops, and the judge of Bukhara 'Amir ibn 'Imran with the people of Bukhara, came out (of Bukhara) in the month of Rajab of the year 159 (April 776). They went to the village of Narshakh, now called Narjaq, and there pitched camp opposite them (the "White Raiments"). The judge of Bukhara said, "I shall preach to them the true faith, for we should not fight with them." So the judge entered the village, accompanied by people of integrity, to turn them back to the true faith. They replied, "We do not know what you are saying." Every day they increased their unbelief and would not accept admonition.

Then they joined in battle. The first man to attack them (the "White Raiments") was an Arab called Na'im ibn Sahl. He fought long and killed a number of people and finally was himself killed. The "White Raiments" were defeated and seven hundred of them were killed. The rest fled and the day came to an end. When it was morning they sent a messenger and asked for amnesty. They said, "We have become Muslims." Peace was made with them, and a peace treaty was written. Provisions were made forbidding them to molest the roads or to kill Muslims, and for them to disperse to their villages and obey their amir. They confirmed their faith in God and His Prophet. All of the notables of the city signed that treaty. When the Muslims had withdrawn, the (White Raiments) broke the treaty. They again severed the highways and killed Muslims. They brought into the fortress of Narshakh the unripened ears of grain (of the Muslims), and the position of the Muslims became critical.

Mahdi, who was the caliph, sent his prime minister Jibra'll ibn Yahya to fight Muqanna'. He came to Bukhara and pitched camp before the Samarqand gate, before going to fight Muqanna'. Husain ibn Mu'adh went to him and said, "Give me aid in fighting with the "White Raiments" (here), so that when we finish with this business I can go with you to fight Muqanna'." Jibra'il consented. He broke camp and went to the village of Narshakh and ordered a ditch dug around the village. He pitched camp in the moat and ordered the troops to be vigilant so that the "White Raiments" could not come out and attack at night. It happened just as he said. They came out the first night, made an assault and inflicted great loss. When Husain ibn Mu'adh, the amir of Bukhara, saw that he thanked Jibral'il very much and said, "Stay in Bukhara and do not go to Kesh till the work is finished here." Jibra'il joined in the fray, and fought continuously for four months morning and evening.

The "White Raiments" were victorious every day and the Muslims were helpless. They sought for a ruse. Malik ibn Hazim said, "I propose a plan." He ordered a tunnel dug from the camping ground to the wall of the fortress. He sent armed men into it and ordered all that was dug out to be made strong with wood, reeds, and earth, and kept covered till they came under the walls of the fortress. (He ordered) an area of fifty gaz (cubit) by measure to be excavated and strengthened with pillars. When a space of fifty gaz had been dug they filled it full of fire wood and poured oil on it. They set fire to it so the pillars would burn and the walls of the fortress would collapse. But the fire would not start, for a wind was necessary to make the fire burn and there was no way for the wind to blow into the fortress. They set up and prepared catapults against that tower under which (the tunnel) had been dug. They hurled stones and made a breach. The wind found a way and it began to burn. The pillars burned and the (walls), for an extent of fifty gaz, fell down. The Muslims wielded their swords and killed many people.

The remainder asked for a truce and they concluded an agreement on the same conditions they had made at first-not to cause trouble to Muslims, to return to their villages, to send their chiefs to the caliph, and not to carry arms on themselves. They concluded a treaty on these conditions and came out of the village. They crossed the trench, but they had concealed weapons. Jibra'il entrusted their chief Hakim to his son 'Abbas, and he told his son to let Hakim sit in the curtained court and to kill him secretly. They obeyed his order. They brought him to the court, and stood at a distance. Jibra'il went to his curtained court. The "White Raiments" sent Khishwi, who was a friend of Hakim, to Jibra'il to tell him they would not go without Hakim. Khishwi was wearing new boots. He was talking when 'Abbas son of Jibra'il returned and said, "I have killed Hakim." Jibra'il ordered Khishwi pulled from his horse and killed immediately. The "White Raiments" raised a cry and brought out their weapons, and a battle began. Jibra'il ordered his troops all to mount and enter into battle. The struggle was more obstinate than before. They fought fiercely and finally a second time they suffered defeat. A large number of them were killed, and those who remained fled.

The head of the village of Narshakh was a woman whose husband was called Sharaf. He had been a captain of Abu Muslim, and the latter had killed him. This woman was brought to Jibra'il, and with her a blind cousin, who was very foul and wicked. Jibra'il said to that woman, "Pardon Abu Muslim." She replied, "Abu Muslim is called the father of Muslims. He who killed my husband cannot be the father." Jibra'il ordered the woman cut in two parts and her cousin also put to death.

Kirdik went to Muqanna' but Baghi, who was also one of them, was killed in battle. Jibra'il brought their heads (of the dead "White Raiments") to Sughd to frighten the "White Raiments" in Sughd. The people of Sughd had an amir of the leaders of Muqanna' called Sughdiyan. The people of Sughd supported him and Jibra'il had to fight many times with the inhabitants of Sughd. Finally a man of Bukhara killed Sughdiyan, and that group was dispersed.

Jibra'il went thence to Samarqand where he fought much with the Turks and the "White Raiments" till Mu'adh ibn Muslim became the amir of Khurasan. The latter came to Merv in the year 161/777–8 and began activity from there. He passed through the desert of Amui. When he arrived at Bukhara, from the people of Bukhara [the farmers], 570,000 (*sic*) warriors were assembled. Mu'adh ibn Muslim ordered many implements of war made. He made ready three thousand workers equipped with axes, spades, buckets, and hatchets, and also all sorts of artisans who are useful in an army. He built catapults and ballistae, and with the best (possible) organization he moved towards Sughd. In Sughd there were many "White Raiments" and many Turkish troops had come.

The amir of Herat had brought 10,000 sheep from Herat, which were all with him. Mu'adh ibn Muslim told him, "Here the Turks, our adversaries, are near, and they love sheep very much. Send these sheep to Bukhara, or sell them to me so I may divide them among the troops." He did not consent to do either. A troop of Turks came, attacked, and carried away all of those sheep to a place between Arbinjan and Zarman. The troops went in pursuit of them. Some (of the Turks) were killed and they ('Abbasid forces) returned. Mu'adh ibn Muslim went to Sughd and Samarqand and fought a great deal with the Turks and the "White Raiments." In the course of two years sometimes he was victorious and sometimes his enemies. After two years he requested retirement and Musaiyab ibn Zuhair al-Dabbi became the amir of Khurasan in Merv on Jumada 'l-'Ula of the year 163 (January–February, 780). In the month of Rajab (March–April) he came to Bukhara. The amir of Bukhara was Junaid ibn Khalid. The amir of Khurasan sent him to Khwarazm.

In Bukhara there was a captain of Muqanna' called Kular Tekin with an army and a guard prepared. (The amir) had to fight with him.

Muhammad ibn Ja'far has related that 50,000 men of the army of Muqanna', composed of the people of Transoxiana, the Turks, and others, gathered at the gate of the fortress of Muqanna' and prostrated themselves and cried that they wanted a sight of him. They received no answer. Then they entreated him and said, "We shall not leave if we do not obtain a view of our lord." (Muqanna') had a slave called Hajib. Muqanna' told him, "Tell my followers <ashes in his mouth> that Moses requested a sight of me. I did not show myself to him for he did not have the power (to endure it). He who sees me cannot stand it and dies instantly." They remonstrated and increased their demand, and said, "We want a sight (of him). If we perish it doesn't matter." He promised them that on a certain day, if they came, he would show himself to them. Then he issued commands to the women who were with him in the fortress. There were one hundred of the daughters of the *dihqans* of Sughd, Kesh and Nakhshab, whom he had with him.

He had a custom that wherever there was a beautiful woman, she was shown to him, and he brought her to live with him. There was no one in the castle except these women and that particular slave. Whatever food they needed was brought to the fortress once every day. Outside there was an agent who brought whatever was necessary. The slave requested it from him and brought it into the castle. No one had seen his (Muqanna's) hideous face for he wore a green veil on his face.

Then he ordered the women, each to take a mirror and climb to the roof of the castle. Then they were to hold them next to one another at the time the sunlight struck the ground. They were to take all of the mirrors in their hands and hold them together without a space between. A crowd gathered. When the sunlight fell on those mirrors the area was filled with light from the reflection of the mirrors. Then he told the slave to tell his followers that God is showing his face to them, and look! They looked and saw all of the world full of light.

They became afraid and all in one motion prostrated themselves. They said, "Oh lord! this glory and power, which we
saw, is enough. If we see more of this we shall perish from
fear." They remained prostrated till Muqanna' ordered his
slave to tell his followers to raise their heads, for their lord is
pleased with them and forgives their sins. That group raised
their heads from prostration with fear and fright. Then he said,
"I grant you all districts, and the life, possessions, and children
of him who does not join me, are legal for you." <Ashes in his
mouth.> From there that group turned to plundering and they
boasted to others, "We have seen God."

XXVIII

The cause of the destruction of Muqanna'

Sa'id, the amir of Herat, was encamped at the gate of his (Muqanna's) fortress with a large army. He had houses and baths constructed and remained there summer and winter. Inside the fortress was a spring of water, trees, and sown fields. His (Muqanna's) close associates and generals, with a powerful army, were in the fortress. In the fortress was a castle on top of a hill, and no one was allowed to enter that castle. He stayed in the castle with his women. He had the custom of eating and drinking wine every day with those women. So he passed fourteen years in this manner. When the amir of Herat made his situation critical, and his forces became scattered, the general who was in the fortress opened the gate and came out to submit. He accepted Islam. The Muslims seized the fortress and Muqanna' knew he could not hold out in the inner castle.

Muhammad ibn Ja'far related (a story) from Abu 'Ali Muhammad ibn Harun, a *dihqan* of Kesh, who said his grandmother was one of the group of women whom Muqanna' had taken for himself and held in the castle. She related "One day Muqanna' had his women sit, eat, and drink as was his custom.

He put poison in the wine. He ordered each woman (to take) a separate cup and said, 'When I drink my cup you must all drink yours.' Then all drank except me. I poured it in my collar and he did not realize it. All the women fell down and died. I also threw myself among them and feigned death, so he did not know my condition. Then Muqanna' rose, looked and saw all of his women dead. He went to his slave, struck with his sword, and cut off his head.

He had ordered an oven heated for three days. He approached the oven, took off his robe and threw himself into the oven. Then smoke came out. I went over to that oven and saw no trace of him. There was no one alive in that castle. The reason for his burning himself alive was that he used to say, 'When my followers become rebellious I shall go to heaven to bring angels to chastise them.' He burned himself so the people would say that he had gone to heaven to bring angels, to give them assistance from the sky, so his faith would remain in the world. Then that woman opened the gate of the fortress and Sa'id Harashi entered and seized his treasury.

Ahmad ibn Muhammad ibn Nasr says that those people still remain in the districts of Kesh and Nakhshab and some of the villages of Bukhara, like the castle of 'Umar, the castle of Khakhushtuvan and the village of Zarman. They themselves have no knowledge about Muqanna', but they accept his faith. Their religion is such that they neither pray, nor fast, nor do they wash after sexual intercourse. Still they remain in safety, and concealing all of those conditions from the Muslims, they claim to be Muslims. It is said that they allow their women free for one another. They say a woman is like a flower, (no matter) who smells it, nothing is detracted from it. When a man comes to a woman in private he puts a mark on the door of the house, so when the husband of this woman arrives he knows that this woman is in the house with a man. He goes away and when the other man is finished he returns to his home. They have a chief in each village whom they obey.

Story: It is said that they have a man in each village who, whenever anyone wants to take a virgin in marriage, first destroys her virginity, and after that surrenders her to her husband, Ahmad ibn Muhammad ibn Nasr says, "I asked the elders of the village what was the sense of allowing such great pleasure to this one man, while the rest were deprived of it. They said that their rule was that every youth who reached maturity should satisfy his need with this person until he should marry a woman. His repayment for that was that the wife should remain with him the first night. When this man became old, another would be appointed in his place. The men of the village continually have dealings with this man. The name of such a person who does this work is *thkana*." I do not know if this affair is true. I heard this story from the elders of the village, and from the inhabitants who live in these villages. May God preserve us from that.

XXIX

An account of the beginning of the rule of the Samanid family, may God show mercy on them

It has been mentioned before that Saman Khudah had a son whom he named Asad, out of friendship for Asad ibn 'Abdallah al-Qushairi. Asad had four sons, Nuh, Ahmad, Yahya, and Ilyas. When Rafi' ibn Lakh revolted against Harun al-Rashid and seized Samarqand, Harun al-Rashid sent Harthama ibn A'yan to fight him. Rafi' fortified Samarqand and Harthama was unable to do anything. Ma'mun had come with Harun al-Rashid to Khurasan because of this affair. Harun was very concerned about this difficulty. Ma'mun wrote a letter to the sons of Asad and ordered them to aid Harthama in the war against Rafi'. The sons of Asad induced Rafi' to make peace with Harthama. Marriage alliances were made between them, and Harun was freed from that worry. There was a danger that Rafi' would seize all of Khurasan. This outcome was considered good fortune by Ma'-mun. On this trip Harun died at Tus (*sic*).

When the caliphate passed to Ma'mun, Ghassan ibn 'Abbad became the amir of Khurasan. Ma'mun ordered him to give the children of Asad ibn Saman Khudah districts (to rule) among the cities of Khurasan. He gave each an important city in recognition of what they had done. Ghassan ibn 'Abbad made Nuh ibn Asad the amir of Samarqand and Ahmad ibn Asad the amir of Merv. This was in the year 202/817–818. When Ghassan was recalled from Khurasan, Tahir ibn al-Husain became the amir and confirmed these districts on them. He gave a robe of honor to Nuh ibn Asad the eldest, who was in Samarqand till he died. He (Nuh) made his brother Ahmad ibn Asad his successor. Ahmad ibn Asad was a learned and pious man. He lived in Samarqand until he died. He (Ahmad) named his son, Nasr ibn Ahmad ibn Asad, his successor. When he sat in his father's place there came a mandate from the caliph Wathiq bi'llah (*sic*) for (the rule of) the provinces of Transoxiana, in his name. The date was Saturday the first of the month of Ramadan of the year 251/(Wednesday, September 26, 865; *sic*—261/875).

XXX

The beginning of the rule of the late amir Abu Ibrahim Isma'il ibn Ahmad al-Samani

He was the first ruler of the Samanids. He was really a worthy ruler, meritorious, intelligent, just, kind, and a man of vision and foresight. He always showed obedience to the caliphs and he found it proper and necessary to submit to them. On Saturday, in the middle of Rabi the second of the year 287 (April 900), he took 'Amr (ibn) Laith prisoner at Balkh, and conquered his kingdom. He ruled for a period of eight years. In the year 295/907 he died in Bukhara [*lit.*—he joined the nearness of the mercy of God]. <May God show him mercy and forgive his sins.>

He was born in Ferghana in the month of Shauwal 234 (May 849). When he was sixteen years old his father died. The amir Nasr, who was his elder brother, held him in high esteem. He served the amir Nasr. When Husain ibn Tahir al-Ta'i came to Bukhara from Khwarazm in Rabi the second of the year 260 (January 874), fighting occurred between him and the people of Bukhara. After five days he secured possesion of the city. He

made the people of Bukhara forsake city and village. He killed
many people. He allowed the Khwarazmians to plunder and
confiscate. At night they broke into the houses by force. They
committed serious crimes and seized property. The people of
Bukhara came out to fight against them, and many people were
killed. A third part of the city burned. When the inhabitants
of the city began to prevail, he (Husain) made a proclamation
and made peace. When the people who had gathered and had
engaged in battle heard the news of the peace, they dispersed.
Some went to their villages. When Husain ibn Tahir realized
that the people had dispersed he wielded his sword and killed a
great many people.

The struggle began again and Husain ibn Tahir was defeated. They fought the entire day. When it became night he
fortified the gate of a castle. A group watched the gate of the castle so as to catch him (Husain). He had seized the entire tax of
Bukhara, all in Ghidrifi *dirhams*. He had them piled in the court
and wanted to convert (melt) them all to silver but did not have
time. At night he made a hole in the wall and fled with his followers, destitute and hungry. The Ghidrifi *dirhams* remained (in
the castle). The people heard of this and entered and plundered
that property. Many people became rich from these possessions,
and the residue remained with their children. It was said in the
city that such a one became rich from the court of Husain ibn
Tahir.

After he had fled all of the people of Bukhara had many
quarrels and clashes among themselves. The learned and up-
right people of Bukhara gathered about Abu 'Abdallah the
jurist, son of Khwaja Abu Hafs the great. He was a fighter.
They consulted him regarding the affairs of Bukhara. There
was no amir in Khurasan, for Ya'qub ibn Laith had seized
Khurasan by force and Rafi' ibn Harthama was fighting against
him. There were other disturbances in Khurasan and Bukhara
was being destroyed by these evils. Then Abu 'Abdallah, son of
Khwaja Abu Hafs, wrote a letter to Samarqand to Nasr ibn
Ahmad ibn Asad al-Samani, who was the amir of Samarqand
and Ferghana, and requested an amir for Bukhara from him.

He sent his brother Isma'il ibn Ahmad, to Bukhara. When the amir Isma'il came to Karmina he remained there several days and sent a messenger to Bukhara to Husain ibn Muhammad al-Khawariji, who was (then) the amir of Bukhara. His messenger went several times and returned before it was decided that the amir Isma'il should be amir of Bukhara and Husain ibn Muhammad al-Khawariji his successor. His (Khawar-iji's) army gave allegiance on this condition. Amir Isma'il sent a diploma of successorship to Khawariji with a banner and robe of honor. Khawariji went throughout the city with the banner and robe, and the people of the city rejoiced. This was on a Tuesday, and on Friday the *khutba* was read in the name of Nasr ibn Ahmad. The name of Ya'qub (ibn) Laith was struck out before Amir Isma'il's entry into the city. That (occurred) on the first Friday of the blessed month of Ramadan of the year 260 (ca. 25 June 874). The son of Khwaja Abu Hafs the great <may God bless them both> came out to meet him. With him were all of the nobles of Bukhara, both Arabs and natives, and they came with him to Karmina. Abu Abdallah ordered the city decorated.

Amir Isma'il regretted that he had come to Bukhara without a large retinue, for Bukhara was in turmoil and a riot had begun. He did not know how the people of Bukhara felt (in their hearts) towards him. When Abu 'Abdallah ibn Khwaja Abu Hafs came out and went to Karmina his (Isma'il's) heart was calmed. He knew that whatever Abu 'Abdallah did the people of the city would not go against him. His resolution was strengthened. Abu 'Abdallah praised him very much, and his heart was soothed. When he was brought into the city they showed him honor and respect. He (Abu 'Abdallah) ordered the people of the city to scatter much gold and silver on him. Amir Isma'il seized Husain al-Khawariji and sent him to prison. The strife ceased by the power of God the Exalted.

XXXI

The entry of the amir Isma'il into Bukhara

It was on Monday, the twelfth day of the blessed month of Ramadan of the year 260 (*ca.* 1 July 874). Because of this the city was quiet and the people of Bukhara were delivered from trouble and enjoyed peace. In the same year the amir Nasr ibn Ahmad was sent a diploma for the rule of all of the districts of Transoxiana, from the Oxus river to the extremity of the lands of the East, from the caliph Muwaffaq bi'llah. The *khutba* of Bukhara was read in the names of the amir Nasr ibn Ahmad and the amir Isma'il, and the name of Ya'qub (ibn) Laith Saffar was dropped from the *khutba*. Amir Isma'il lived some time in Bukhara and after that went to Samarqand, without waiting for an order from the amir Nasr. He left his nephew Abu Zakarlya Yahya ibn Ahmad ibn Asad as his deputy in Bukhara. When he arrived in Rishkhan (*sic* Rabinjan) the amir Nasr received news and became angry at his coming without permission. He ordered him (Isma'il) to be received but himself did not come out. He did not honor him, but ordered him escorted to the fortress of Samarqand. The chief of police of Samarqand rep-

resented him (Nasr). Thus he (Nasr) showed his displeasure at
him. Amir Isma'il went to greet him (Nasr) because he had not
done so since his departure to Bukhara. Muhammad ibn 'Umar
was made his (Nasr's) deputy. Amir Isma'il came with greeting
and remained standing an hour; then he left. Amir Nasr did not
speak a word with him.

It was like this for thirteen months. (Isma'il) had his cousin
Muhammad ibn Nuh and 'Abd al-Jabbar ibn Hamza intercede
for him, to send him back to Bukhara. He (Nasr) appointed
'Ismat ibn Muhammad al-Marvazi his (Isma'il's) chief minister
and Fadl ibn Ahmad al-Marvazi his secretary. Amir Nasr, with
all of his principal chiefs and friends in Samarqand, came out to
bid farewell to Isma'il. At this interval the amir Nasr turned his
face towards 'Abd al-Jabbar ibn Hamza, and said, "Oh Abu'l-
Fath! I am sending this youth, what may I expect of him?"
'Abd al-Jabbar said, "Do not speak thus, for he is your servant.
Whatever you order the amir Isma'il will do it and will never
oppose you. I speak the truth." Then he added, "What is your
opinion?" Amir Nasr replied, "In his eyes and disposition I see
rebellion and disobedience." When the amir Isma'il arrived at
Bukhara the inhabitants received him and brought him in the
city with full honors.

A thief had gathered around him a group of ruffians and
rogues of the villages; four thousand men had been assembled.
They cut the road between Ramitin and Barkad, and had almost begun to attack the city. Amir Isma'il sent Husain ibn
al-'Ala, his chief of police, to fight these thieves. He had built
the walls of Bukhara, and the quarter of 'Ala was named after
him. The nobles and chiefs of Bukhara aided him. They fought
the thieves and defeated them. Husain ibn al-'Ala obtained victory. He captured the most important of the thieves, killed him
and brought back his head. He also captured a large number
who had followed him. The amir Isma'il bound them and sent
them to Samarqand.

When this affair was finished, news arrived that Husain ibn
Tahir had come with two thousand men to Amui with the intention (of attacking) Bukhara. Amir Isma'il assembled as much of

an army as he could and went to battle. News came that Husain ibn Tahir had crossed the Oxus with two thousand Khwarazmi-ans. Amir Isma'il mounted, advanced, and they fought a fierce battle. Husain ibn Tahir was defeated and some of his troops were killed and others drowned in the river. Seventy men were taken captive. This was the first war of the amir Isma'il. When it was morning the amir (Isma'il) summoned the captives, gave each one a cotton garment, and dismissed them.

Husain ibn Tahir went to Merv and the amir Isma'il returned to Bukhara and investigated the state of the kingdom. He found that the nobles of Bukhara did not show him sufficient honor. There was no respect in their eyes and their gathering together did not portend good for him. So he resolved on the following good course of action. He addressed a group of the prominent people of Bukhara and said, "You must go to Samarqand on my behalf and speak to the amir Nasr, to request pardon for me." They replied, "We hear and obey." They asked several days respite before they left. This group was composed of former amirs of Bukhara, before the amir Isma'il. Abu Muhammad Bukhar Khudah himself had been ruler of Bukhara, and Abu Hatim Yasari was very wealthy. Because of their great wealth they were disobedient. The nobles of Bukhara went with these two to Samarqand. Amir Isma'il wrote a letter to the amir Nasr to imprison them, so he could consolidate the rule of Bukhara. Amir Nasr did that and retained those people there for some time until he (Isma'il) quieted Bukhara. Amir Isma'il again sent a letter to the amir Nasr and sought their release. After that the amir Isma'il was friendly to them and fulfilled their needs. He saw the propriety of his fulfilling their just dues.

Nasr ibn Ahmad had stipulated from Isma'il 500,000 *dirhams* a year of the income of Bukhara. After (Isma'il) had to fight, he spent the money and could not send (that amount) any more. Amir Nasr sent messengers for that money, but he (Isma'il) did not send it. Because of this strife appeared between them. Amir Nasr collected an army and wrote a letter to Ferghana, to his brother Abul-Ash'ath requesting him to come with a large army. He wrote another letter to Shash, to another brother, Abu Yusuf

Ya'qub ibn Ahmad, to come with his army, and to bring the Turks of Istijab (*sic* Isfijab). A large army assembled.

He set out for Bukhara in the month of Rajab of the year 272 (December 885). When the amir Isma'il heard of it he evacuated Bukhara and went to Farab out of respect for his brother. Amir Nasr came to Bukhara. When he did not find the amir Isma'il he went to Baikand and remained there. The people of Baikand received him. They showered gold and silver on him and brought out many gifts. There was friendship between the amir Isma'il and Rafi' ibn Harthama, who at that time was the amir of Khurasan. Amir Isma'il wrote him a letter and requested help from him. Rafi' came with his army. The Oxus was frozen and he crossed on the ice. When the amir Nasr received news of the coming of Rafi' he returned to Bukhara.

Amir Isma'il agreed with Rafi' to go and capture Samarqand. This news came to Nasr and he quickly went to Tawais and blocked the way. Amir Isma'il and Rafi' went by the desert route. All of the villages of Bukhara were in the possession of the amir Nasr. They did not find any food or forage in the desert. There was a famine that year, and it was very difficult for them, so that a man of bread in their army cost three dirhams. A large number of Rafi's troops perished from hunger. Amir Nasr wrote to his son Ahmad in Samarqand to gather volunteers from Sughd of Samarqand. The people of the district did not give the amir Isma'il fodder. They said, "These are rebels. It is not lawful for us to give them aid." Yet the amir Nasr, because of the coming of Rafi', was discouraged. He went to Karmina, and they (Isma'il and Rafi') followed him.

A person gave counsel to Rafi' and said, "You left your territory and came here. If the two brothers become reconciled and attack you between them, what can you do?" Rafi', hearing these words, began to be afraid. He sent a messenger to the amir Nasr and said, "I did not come for war, but to reconcile you." Amir Nasr was pleased with these words and they made peace on the condition that the amir of Bukhara would be another person, while the amir Isma'il would be the revenue collector. The affairs of the chancellery and the *khutba* would not be in his name. Every year he would have to send 500,000 *dirhams*. He (Rafi') saluted the amir Nasr ibn Ahmad, as well as Ishaq ibn Ahmad. He (Nasr) gave the latter a robe of honor, and also gave him the governorship of Bukhara. Amir Isma'il agreed to that. Amir Nasr returned (to Samarqand), while Rafi' also left for Khurasan. This was in the year 273/886.

Fifteen months after this event, the amir Nasr sent a man to obtain the money. Amir Isma'il held back the money and did not send it. Amir Nasr then sent a letter to Rafi', for the latter had given surety. Rafi' also wrote a letter to the amir Isma'il in this sense. Amir Isma'il did not pay any attention to it. Amir Nasr again collected an army, all from the inhabitants of Transoxiana. Abu'l-Ash'ath came from Ferghana, and they went towards Bukhara again, just as before. They advanced and when they arrived in Karmina the amir Isma'il also gathered his army and went to Tawais.

They joined in battle, and the conflict was stubborn. Ishaq ibn Ahmad fled in defeat to Farab. Amir Isma'il made a strong attack on the people of Ferghana and Abu'l Ash'ath fled in defeat to Samarqand. The people of Samarqand wanted to seize him because he had abandoned his brother and fled. (So) Abu 'l-Ash'ath returned from Samarqand and came to Rabinjan. Amir Isma'il made Ahmad ibn Musa Marzuq prisoner and sent him to Bukhara. The army of Bukhara was again defeated. Amir Isma'il remained on the spot with only a small number of followers. Among the well-known with him was Sima' 1-Kabir. Amir Isma'il sent a man to collect all of the slaves and clients who had fled. He brought Ishaq ibn Ahmad (his brother) back from Farab. Two thousand volunteers came from Bukhara and a strong army assembled. He gave all of them rations.

Amir Nasr went to Rabinjan, prepared his army, and returned. Amir Isma'il went before him to a village Wazbdin. They assembled there and joined battle on Tuesday, the fifteenth day of the month of the second Jumada of the year 275 (26 October 888). Amir Isma'il was victorious over the army of Ferghana and Abu'l-Ash'ath fled in defeat. The entire army was defeated. Amir Nasr remained with a few men, but he too was defeated.

Amir Isma'il called to a group of Khwarazmians to keep away from the amir Nasr; then he (Isma'il) descended from his horse and kissed his (Nasr's) stirrup.

Sima'l-Kabir had been a slave of their father, and was (Isma'il's) commander-in-chief. He received the news and sent a person to inform Isma'il. Nasr ibn Ahmad dismounted from his horse, put down a cushion and sat on it. Amir Isma'il arrived and jumped off his horse, came to Nasr and kissed the cushion and said, "Oh amir! This was the will of God which made me (victorious) over you. I see His great work today with my own eyes." Amir Nasr replied, "I was surprised at what you did, since you did not obey your amir and did not observe the mandate which God the Exalted placed on you." Amir Isma'il said, "Oh amir, I acknowledge that I committed an error, and it is all my fault. You are better (than I) in kindness, so that you will let pass this great sin, and forgive me."

They were speaking thus when another brother, Ishaq ibn Ahmad arrived and did not dismount from his horse. Amir Isma'il said, "Oh fellow, why don't you dismount (before) your superior?" He scolded him and was angry at him. Ishaq quickly dismounted and fell at Nasr's feet. He kissed the ground and asked forgiveness, (saying), "My horse was unmanageable and I could not dismount quickly."

When these words were finished the amir Isma'il said, "Oh amir, it is best that you quickly return to your home before news of this arrives there and your subjects in Transoxiana revolt." Amir Nasr asked, "Oh Abu Ibrahim, are you going to send me back to my place?" Isma'il replied, "If I do not do this what should I do? (Between) a slave and his master no other arrangement is possible. Whatever you wish (is yours)." Amir Nasr spoke and tears rolled down his cheek. He repented that he had embarked (on the war) and the blood which had been spilt. Then he rose and mounted (his horse). Amir Isma'il and his brother Ishaq held the stirrups and sent him on his way. He sent Sima'l-Kabir and 'Abdallah ibn Muslim as escorts. They went one march and the amir Nasr sent them back while he continued to Samarqand. On the same day that Nasr ibn Ahmad had been made a prisoner, he spoke to that group (the people of Samarqand) in the same (manner) as when he was the amir. He sat on the throne and they stood in service before him. Four years later the amir Nasr died, seven days before the end of the month of Jumada the first of the year 279 (21 August 892). He named the amir Isma'il his successor over all of the provinces of Transoxiana. He placed another brother, and his own son, under him (Isma'il).

When the amir Nasr died the amir Isma'il went from Bukhara to Samarqand and brought the kingdom in order. He appointed his (Nasr's) son Ahmad ibn Nasr his deputy (in Samarqand). He undertook raiding expeditions from there. Amir Isma'il returned to Bukhara, and he had been there twenty years before his brother died and gave all of Transoxiana to him.

When the news of the death of the amir Nasr came to the Commander of the Faithful Mu'tadid bi'llah, (279–289/ 892–902) he gave the amir Isma'il a mandate for the dominion of Transoxiana in the month of Muharram of 280 (March or April 893). At the same time he (Isma'il) went to fight at Taraz, where he experienced great difficulty. Finally the amir of Taraz came out with many *dihqans* and accepted Islam. Taraz was thus subjugated. A large church was transformed into a grand mosque, and the *khutba* was read in the name of the Commander of the Faithful Mu'tadid bi'llah. Amir Isma'il returned to Bukhara with much booty.

He ruled seven years and was the amir of Transoxiana at the time Amr (ibn) Laith became powerful and seized a part of Khurasan, and began to make raids. 'All ibn Husain, the amir (of Merv) requested help from Ahmad, the amir of Guzganiyan, but not receiving a favorable answer, he crossed the Oxus and came to the amir Isma'il in Bukhara. The amir was pleased and went out to meet him with troops, and with great honor and respect he brought him to Bukhara and sent him many gifts. 'Ali ibn Husain went to Farab (from Bukhara) and remained there thirteen months. Amir Isma'il continually sent gifts to him and held him in esteem. 'Ali ibn Husain remained there till his (Isma'il's?) son killed him in battle.

'Amr (ibn) Laith sent a letter to Abu Daud, the amir of Balkh, to Ahmad ibn Farighun, the amir of Guzganiyan, and to the amir Isma'il of Transoxiana calling on them to submit to him. He offered good treaties. The (first two) went at his command and entered his service. A messenger came to the amir Isma'il and gave him a letter. He told of the submission of the amirs of Balkh and Guzganiyan, and said, "You are more powerful and worthy of giving submission, for you know the worth of impe- rial dignity as you (were born) a prince." Amir Isma'il answered, "Is your master so ignorant that he placed me on the same level as them? They are my subjects. My answer to you is with the sword. There can only be war between us. Return and tell him to prepare the weapons of war."

'Amar (ibn) Laith consulted his amirs and nobles and re- quested aid from them in the affair with the amir Isma'il. He said, "Another person must be sent to speak peacefully. We must give him good conditions." Then he sent (to Isma'il) a group of the elders of Nishapur and some of his nobles. He wrote a let- ter in which it was recalled, "Although the Commander of the Faithful has given me this territory, I make you a partner in the rule. You must be friendly to me and regard me well so there will be no dispute between us. Let friendship and harmony exist between us. Whatever I have previously said was from rashness. I have passed over that. You must guard the province of Trans- oxiana which is the boundary to the enemy. (You must also) take care of your subjects. I confer that province on you, and wish you only prosperity and thriving, not your house and posses- sions." He sent some of the notables of Nishapur. He went to his father's (grave), swore an oath and made them his confidents. He continued, "I trust no one except you (amir Isma'il). You must have faith in me and make a covenant with me, so our friendship will be strengthened."

When news of 'Amr (ibn) Laith came to the amir (Isma'il) he sent (soldiers) to the bank of the river, not to allow them (the envoys) to cross. Whatever had been brought by them was nei- ther received nor transmitted (to Isma'il). It was sent back with scorn. 'Amr (ibn) Laith became angry and prepared for war. He ordered 'Ali ibn Surush (*sic*: Sharvin), his general, to go with an army to Amuya, to halt there and not to make haste to cross until he was ordered. He sent after him another general Muhammad ibn Laith with 5,000 men. He told him (Muhammad) to take counsel with 'Ali ibn Surush and hold back the army. "Whoever comes from there (Bukhara) for peace, give it and treat him well. Prepare boats and send out scouts."

'Amr (ibn) Laith continued to send troops. When the amir Isma'il heard of this he hastened from Bukhara with 20,000 men and came to the bank of the Oxus. He made a surprise move and crossed the Oxus at night. 'Ali ibn Surush heard of this, quickly mounted and armed his troops. He sent the infantry ahead and they began the battle. The army of the amir Isma'il attacked from all sides and the struggle was fierce. Muhammad ibn 'Ali ibn Surush retreated and was captured. Many of the notables of Nishapur were also taken prisoner. The next day the amir Isma'il (treated) the troops of 'Amr (ibn) Laith kindly, gave them provisions, and sent them back to 'Amr (ibn) Laith. The chiefs of the army of Isma'il said, "How can you give garments and send back those who fought against us and were captured?" Amir Isma'il replied, "What do you want from these unfortunates? Allow them to go to their country and they will never fight against you again. They will influence the hearts of others." Amir Isma'il returned to Bukhara with much silver, clothes, gold and weapons.

After that 'Amr (ibn) Laith remained a year in Nishapur in melancholy and sorrow, grief, and remorse. He used to say, "I want revenge for Ali (ibn) Surush and his son. When the amir Isma'il received news that 'Amr (ibn) Laith was preparing for war, he gathered his army. He gave them rations and moved against them (the foe) from all sides. He gave rations to the capable and the unfit, even to scoundrels; he gave rations to all. The population became discontent at this. They said, "Does he expect to fight 'Amr (ibn) Laith with this army?"

Information of this came to 'Amr (ibn) Laith and he became happy. He (Isma'il) was on the bank of the Oxus. Mansur Qaratekin and Pars Baikandi came to Amuya from Khwarazm.

Thirty thousand men arrived from Turkistan and Ferghana. On the twenty-fifth of Dhu'l Qa'da he (Isma'il) sent Muhammad ibn Harun with the advance guard of the army. The next day he himself left and crossed the Oxus. Troops from all sides gathered at Amuya. From Bukhara they went to a city of Khwarazm (*sic*) and prepared (for war) till the following Monday. From there they went towards Balkh. 'Amr (ibn) Laith undertook the fortification of the town and encamped with his army before the city (proper). He made a moat all around (the city). It was several days before the army entered (the city) and he strengthened the fortifications. He showed the inhabitants what he had done for their city and made them happy.

Amir Isma'il sent 'Ali ibn Ahmad to Faryab and ordered him to kill the deputies of 'Amr (ibn) Laith, and to bring back much booty. He sent people everywhere to kill the adherents of 'Amr (ibn) Laith. They brought back wealth. Amir Isma'il arrived in 'Aliabad of Balkh and remained there three days. He directed his army from there. He indicated that he wanted to stay at a place of prayer, and he ordered the road (which led to it) widened. When 'Amr (ibn) Laith saw that, he strengthened the gates on that side and stationed troops in that section. He also prepared catapults and ballistae on that side. He laid an ambush on the road to the place of prayer and placed troops in it. When it was morning, the late amir (Isma'il) changed his route and went to the city gate by another route, and descended at the bridge of 'Ata. 'Amr (ibn) Laith was surprised at this act and had to transfer the catapults to the other side.

Amir Isma'il remained there three days. He ordered water cut off from the city; the walls were all cast down, trees were uprooted, and the roads prepared. On Tuesday morning the amir Isma'il mounted, and with a few soldiers went to the city gate. 'Amr (ibn) Laith came out and entered in battle. The battle was fierce and his ('Amr's) army was defeated. The troops (of Isma'il) followed them, killed some and captured others till they arrived eight parasangs from Balkh. They saw 'Amr (ibn) Laith with two bodyguards. One fled and the other fell upon 'Amr. Then 'Amr (ibn) Laith was taken prisoner and everyone said he had captured 'Amr (ibn) Laith, but he said that his bodyguard had seized him. 'Amr (ibn) Laith had given that servant fifteen pearls, each valued at 70,000 *dirhams*. They were taken from the servant.

The capture of 'Amr (ibn) Laith occurred on Wednesday the tenth day of the month of Jumada the first of the year 288 (2 May 901). 'Amr (ibn) Laith was brought before the amir Isma'il. 'Amr (ibn) Laith wanted to dismount but the amir (Isma'il) restrained him and said, "Today I shall do something with you which will amaze the people." He ordered 'Amr (ibn) Laith brought to a tent and he sent his (Isma'il's) brother to guard him. Four days later he saw the amir (Isma'il who) asked him how he fell into captivity. The (former) replied, "I was galloping and my horse became tired. So I dismounted and slept. Then I saw two youths standing by my head. One of them took his whip and touched me on the nose. I said, 'What do you want from such an old man?' I exorcised them not to kill me. They dismounted and kissed my foot. They protected me and one of them put me on his horse. People gathered and asked me what I had. I told them I had several pearls, each valued at 70,000 *dirhams*. I also gave them my ring. They took my shoes from my feet and also they took several jewels of great value. Then troops captured me. Muhammad Shah held back the people from me. Then I saw the amir Isma'il from afar. I wanted to dismount but he entreated me with his heart and soul not to dismount. My heart was calmed. He led me to a curtained tent and Abu Yusuf sat with me and guarded me. When I wanted water they gave me sherbet. Really they showed me all sorts of respect and honor. Then the amir Isma'il came to me, welcomed me, and promised not to kill me. He ordered me carried in a litter and brought to the city (of Samarqand) in honor. I was brought into Samarqand at night so none of the inhabitants knew of this. Amir Isma'il bought my ring from the person who had it. He paid a price of 3,000 *dirhams* and sent it to me. The stone of the ring was a red ruby."

'Amr (ibn) Laith continued, "On the day of the battle I had 40,000 *dirhams* which were lost in the fight. I was on a horse

which could run fifty parasangs. I had tried it many times. On
that day the same horse went so slowly that I wanted to dismount. The horse's legs tripped in a ditch and I fell from the
horse and despaired for myself. When those two (men) came towards me I told that man who was with me to mount my horse
and flee. He mounted the horse, and I watched him go like a
cloud. Then I knew that it was my bad fortune and not the fault
of the horse."

'Amr (ibn) Laith told the amir Isma'il, "I have hidden ten
donkey loads of gold in Balkh. Please order them brought,
for you now are more deserving of them." Amir Isma'il sent
a person and brought all of it. He then sent it to 'Amr (ibn)
Laith. Amir Isma'il, no matter how often requested, accepted
nothing.

A letter from the Commander of the Faithful arrived in
Samarqand requesting that 'Amr (ibn) Laith (be sent). The
heading of the letter was written as follows: "From 'Abdallah
ibn al-Imam abul-'Abbas al-Mu'tadid bi'llah, Commander of
the Faithful, to Abu Ibrahim Isma'il ibn Ahmad, client of the
Commander of the Faithful." When the letter reached the amir
Isma'il he was grieved for the sake of 'Amr (ibn) Laith, but he
was unable to ignore the order of the caliph. He ordered 'Amr
(ibn) Laith placed in a litter and brought to Bukhara. Amir
Isma'il could not even turn his face towards him, because of
shame. He sent a man to ask if he ('Amr) had any wishes. 'Amr
(ibn) Laith said, "Take care of my children and give something
to those persons who carry me so they will think well of me."
Amir Isma'il did that, and seated him in a litter and sent him
to Baghdad. When he arrived in Baghdad the caliph entrusted
him to Safi his servant, and put him in prison. He was imprisoned by Safi till the end of the reign of Mu'tadid. He had been
in prison two years when he was killed in the year 280/893-4,
(*sic* 289/902).

When the amir Isma'il sent Amr (ibn) Laith to the caliph,
the latter sent back the investiture for Khurasan from the pass
of Hulwan, including the provinces of Khurasan, Transoxiana,
Turkestan, Sind, Hind, and Gurgan. All became his, and the

amir appointed an amir over every city. He made appear the results of justice and good conditions. He chastised whoever showed tyranny to his subjects. There was no one of the house of Saman more capable of governing than he, for he was like an ascetic and allowed no favoritism in the affairs of state. He always showed obedience to the caliph. In his lifetime he was not refactory one hour to the caliph, and he held his commands in highest esteem.

Amir Isma'il became sick; it was prolonged and the moisture aggravated his trouble. The doctors said that the atmosphere of Juy-i Muliyan was wet, so he was carried to the village of Zarman, which was his private property. They said that this air would be better for him. The amir liked that village and always went there for hunting. A garden had been made for him. He was sick there for some time till he died. It was in a certain garden under a large tree. It was on the fifteenth day of the month of Safar of the year 295 (26 November 907). He had been the amir of Khurasan twenty years, and the length of his rule was thirty years.< May God show mercy on him>, for in his time Bukhara became the seat of government. After him all of the amirs of the house of Saman held court in Bukhara. None of the amirs of Khurasan before him had lived in Bukhara. He considered his residence in Bukhara as fortunate, and he did not find satisfaction in any district except Bukhara. Wherever he was, he said my city, i.e., Bukhara, (has) such and such. After his death his son took his place, and he (Isma'il) was surnamed al-amir al-madi.

XXXII

The reign of the martyred amir Ahmad ibn Isma'il Samani

He became the amir of Khurasan, and is known as the martyred amir. He followed his father in disposition and was just. He showed equity to all of his subjects, and they lived in peace and tranquility. He went from there (Bukhara) to Khurasan and inspected his kingdom. Then he conquered Sistan, for already in the time of the late amir it had been allotted to him. Then he returned to Bukhara. He loved to hunt, so he went hunting on the bank of the Oxus. He had pitched his tent and had returned from hunting, when a messenger came and brought a letter from Abu'l-'Abbas the amir of Tabaristan. He read the letter. In it was written that Husain (*sic*) ibn 'Ala had revolted and seized most of the provinces of Gurgan and Tabaristan. He (Abu'l-'Abbas) had been obliged to flee. The amir became despondent and very disturbed. He prayed and said, "Great God, if this kingdom is to fall away from me, give me death." (Then) he entered the tent.

He had a rule, viz.—he had a lion which was fastened by a chain at the door of the house where he slept, so if anyone sought to enter the house the lion would destroy him. That night, when he was sad, all of his domestics grieved and forgot to bring the lion. He fell asleep and a group of the amir's slaves entered (the tent) and cut off his head. This happened on Thursday the eleventh of Jumada the second in the year 301 (12 January 914). He was brought to Bukhara and laid in the cemetery of Naukanda. He was designated the martyred amir. It was suspected that Abu'l-Hasan was an accomplice, so he was brought to Bukhara and hanged. Some of the slaves who had killed (the amir) were caught and executed, (while) others fled to Turkistan. His rule lasted six years four months and five days.

XXXIII

The rule of the amir Sa'id abu'l-Hasan Nasr ibn Ahmad ibn Isma'il al-Samani

When they finished with the burial of the martyred amir, his son Nasr received the appellation Sa'id (the fortunate). He was eight years old. Abu Abdallah Muhammad ibn Ahmad al-Jaihani took the post of prime minister, while Hamavaih ibn 'Ali became commander-in-chief of the army. He (Sa'id) was called "he founder of Khurasan." At first the power of the amir Sa'id was weak and everywhere trouble arose. An uncle of his father, Ishaq ibn Ahmad, sought the allegiance of Samarqand, and the people of Samarqand swore allegiance to him. His son Abu Salih Mansur ibn Ishaq revolted in Nishapur and seized several cities of Khurasan. The power of Ishaq ibn Ahmad in Samarqand became strong. Amir Sa'id sent his commander Hamavaih ibn 'All to fight Ishaq. (The latter) was defeated and (the victor's) army entered Samarqand. Ishaq prepared himself a second time and the people of Samarqand came out and joined him. They fought against Hamavaih, but the people of

Samarqand were (again) defeated. Ishaq ibn Ahmad came out a third time and was captured. His son, Mansur ibn Ishaq, died in Nīshapur, and all of Khurasan and Transoxiana was cleared for the amir Sa'id. The *khutba* was said in his name in Fars, Kirman, Tabaristan, Gurgan, and 'Iraq.

Story: In his thirteenth year the amir Sa'id went from Bukhara to Nishapur. He left as his deputy in Bukhara one of his relatives called Abu'l-'Abbas Ahmad ibn Yahya ibn Asad al-Samani. At this time a fire started in the quarter of Gardun Kashan. It was so great that the people of Samarqand saw the fire. The people of Bukhara said that the fire came from heaven. The whole quarter burned, and it was impossible to extinguish it.

On the whole his (the amir's) other brothers revolted and caused much trouble. Finally Abu Zakariya, who was the soul of the trouble, fled with a small number of people, without garments and food, and went to Khurasan. The other brothers asked forgiveness. Amir Sa'id forgave them but kept them near him, so the trouble was quieted.

Story: In the time of the amir Sa'id, Nasr ibn Ahmad ibn Isma'il, in the month of Rajab of the year 325 (May 937), a fire began in Bukhara. All of the bazars were burned. The fire began in a porridge shop at the Samarqand gate. (The man in the shop) picked up the ashes from under the kettle of porridge and carried them to the roof where he had a trough he wanted to fill. An ember was among the ashes, but he didn't know it. The wind carried it to a straw hut and it caught fire. It spread to all of the bazar. The entire quarter of the Samarqand gate burned. The fire was carried in the air like a cloud. The Bakar quarter, the shops of the bazar, the religious school of Farjak, the shops of the shoemakers, the bazar of the money changers, and the cloth dealers, and all on the other side of Bukhara, burned to the edge of the river. The fire jumped over (the river) and caught the mosque of Makh, which was completely burned. The fire burned two days and nights. The people of Bukhara were helpless with it, and had much trouble until they extinguished it on the third day. For one month wood burned under the ashes. More than 100,000 *dirhams* of the people of Bukhara were lost.

They were never able to restore the buildings of Bukhara as they had been previously. Amir Sa'id ruled for thirty-one years. (*Sic*-He ruled twenty-nine years and several months.) He was a just ruler, even more than his father, and he had many merits. If I mentioned all of them it would be too long. When he died his son, Nuh ibn Nasr, came to the throne.

XXXIV

The rule of the amir Hamid abu Muhammad Nuh ibn Nasr ibn Ahmad ibn Isma'il al-Samani

Amir Hamid (the laudable) came to the throne in the first of Sha'ban of the year 331 (April 943). Abu Dharr became his prime minister. He had been a judge of Bukhara. In his time there was no one who knew jurisprudence better than he. The *Mukhtasar-i kafi* was his work. When the amir Sa'id died everyone revolted in every place. Amir Hamid went from Bukhara to Nishapur. Abu 'Ali Isfahani (*sic*) was the amir of Nishapur. (Hamid) ordered him seized, (after which) he pacified the district and scattered the opposition. Then he gave Nishapur to Ibrahim (ibn) Simjur. Abu 'All Isfahani said to himself, "I ruled well over it, and he gave the province to another." Abu 'Ali Isfahani said to Abu Ishaq Ibrahim ibn Ahmad ibn Isma'il al-Samanl, "Go to Bukhara and seize power. If I am with you, the amir (Hamid) will be unable to resist you." Abu Ishaq prepared an army and proclaimed his opposition.

Amir Hamid returned from Nishapur. Abu Ishaq advanced towards him and a battle occurred between them. Amir Hamid was defeated and fled to Bukhara. Abu Ishaq, his uncle, followed him there. On Jumada the second of the year 335 (January 947) all of the people of Bukhara swore allegiance to him, and from all of the minbars of Bukhara the *khutba* was read in the name of Abu Ishaq. After a time he discovered that his army had bad designs on him. They had become reconciled with the amir Hamid and intended to kill him. He left Bukhara and went to Chaganiyan. Amir Hamid gave the commandership of the army to Mansur Qaratekin, and sent him to Merv. He (Mansur) seized 'Ali ibn Muhammad al-Qazvini, (who was governor there) bound him, and sent him to Bukhara, and put an end to that trouble. Amir Hamid, during his reign, fought many battles with everyone who pretended to his throne. By the year 341/952 the provinces had been submitted to the amir Hamid. Amir Hamid died in the month of Rabi the second of the year 343 (August 954). His rule had lasted twelve years.

Ahmad ibn Muhammad ibn Nasr says that Muhammad ibn Ja'far al-Narshakhi wrote his book in his (this amir's) name in the beginning of his reign, in the year 332/943–4. He did not mention completely in his book what had happened in the reign of the amir Hamid. Likewise, that which came after the amir Hamid, of the affairs of the Samani amirs, has been added by me, with the help of God the Exalted.

XXXV

The reign of (the amir Rashid Abu'l-Fawaris) 'Abd al-Malik ibn Nuh ibn Nasr ibn Ahmad ibn Isma'il al-Samani

When the amir Hamid died allegiance was sworn to the amir Rashid (the just), who was ten years old when he ascended the throne. When news of the death of the amir Hamid arrived in the provinces, everyone coveted a district. The amir sent Ash'ath ibn Muhammad ibn Muhammad to Khurasan. He had to fight many times in Herat and Isfahan. He subdued the provinces, and was engaged in that, and fighting battles, when the amir Rashid fell from his horse and died the same night. That night was Wednesday; eight days of the month of Shauwal had passed of the year 350 (20 November 961). He had ruled seven years. When he was buried the army grew restless and revolted. Everyone coveted the kingdom and troubles appeared.

XXXVI

On the reign of Malik Muzaffar abu Salih Mansur ibn Nuh ibn Nasr ibn Ahmad ibn Isma'il al-Samani

Amir Sadid (the correct) ascended the throne and the army swore allegiance to him. Unanimity came after much discussion. They swore allegiance to him on Friday the nineteenth of the month of Shauwal of the year 350 (1 December 961). The commander of the army, Alptekin, was in Nishapur. When news of the death of the amir Rashid reached him he resolved to seize the amir Sadid. The latter sent an army, (so when the army of Alptekin) reached the Oxus and wanted to cross, it could not because a large army had arrived (on the opposite bank). He (Alptekin) wanted to return to his own province of Nishapur. Amir Sadid wrote a letter to Muhammad ibn 'Abd al-Razzaq in Nishapur, not to allow (Alptekin) to enter the city. Alptekin received this information and knew he could not go to Nishapur so he crossed the Oxus by Amui and went to Balkh.

He seized it and raised a rebellion. Amir Sadid sent Ash'ath ibn Muhammad (to fight Alptekin). He fought much and finally drove Alptekin out of Balkh, and the latter went to Ghazna. Ash'ath ibn Muhammad followed him to Ghazna and also fought there. Again Alptekin suffered defeat and fled back to Balkh. Again the amir Sadid gave him amnesty. After this revolt, and much fighting, he returned to (the amir's) service.

At this time the amir Sadid sent many armies to the provinces and cleared the kingdom (of rebels). Rivals no longer existed in the provinces. He conquered the territory of the Dailamites and made peace with them on the condition that every year they send him 150,000 Nishapuri *dirhams*. Amir Sadid died on Sunday the sixteenth of the month of Muharram of the year 365 (25 September, 975). His reign lasted fifteen years and five months. <God knows best.>

XXXVII

An account of the rule of the amir Rashid abu'l-Qasim Nuh ibn Mansur ibn Nuh ibn Nasr ibn Ahmad ibn Isma'il al-Samani

Amir Sadld died on Sunday, and on Monday his son ascended the throne and they swore allegiance to him. Abu 'Abdallah Muhammad ibn Ahmad al-Jaihani was his prime minister, but he asked to be excused because of his age. Several days passed, then the amir made Muhammad ibn 'Abdallah ibn 'Azir his prime minister. The affairs of the kingdom began to flourish. Abu'l-'Abbas Tash was commander of the army, (but) he was removed and Abu'l-Hasan Muhammad ibn Ibrahim became the commander. Abu'l-'Abbas Tash revolted and seized Nishapur. Abu'l-Hasan, the commander, his son Abu 'Ali, and Abu'l-Hasan al-Fa'iq the chamberlain, went to Nishapur and defeated him in the year 377/987. Abu'l-'Abbas fled from Nlshapur to Gurgan where 'Ali ibn Hasan was his friend, and he gave him refuge.

When the commander, Abu'l-Hasan Muhammad ibn Ibrahim, died at the end of the month of Dhu'l Qa'da of the year 378 (March 989) his son became commander. After this the amir Rashid disapproved of him and dismissed him. Abu'l-Hasan al-Fa'iq, the chamberlain, became commander, and went to Herat and fought him (Abu 'Ali). Fa'iq the chamberlain fled from him (Abu 'Ali) and went to Merv in Dhu'l Hijja of the year 378 (April 989). After him Abu'l-Harith Mansur ibn Nuh was governor (of Khurasan) for a year and nine months. Bektuziyan seized him in Sarakhs and the rule of the house of Saman went from there. <God knows best.>

Commentary

Richard N. Frye

The following remarks are general, with few references to sources; for more detailed notes, refer to those in my *The History of Bukhara*, but remember that some require updating, or discarding, in view of new information.

Epithets or appellations were given to rulers in the past, such as Louis the Pious in France, or Richard the Lionheart in England, but in the Middle East it was more widespread and lasted longer. Also an epithet frequently became part of the name, for example the sobriquet Hamid was given to Nuh ibn Nasr, which could be translated as "laudable." Each Samanid ruler had an epithet, which we find in Narshakhi's book.

After the list of prominent judges we find a section on the early history of Bukhara from a book called "The Treasury of the Sciences," which is an unknown work. According to this work the site of the later city was formerly a swamp, which became filled with earth brought by the river of Sogdiana. In early times the main settlement of the oasis was Paikand (Baikand in Arabic) and several villages were settled before the town of Bukhara existed. Paikand was important because it was on high ground where the two rivers (from Samarkand and from Kesh) joined before emptying into the Amu Darya, or later lost in the sands. When settlements grew along both rivers and water was diverted for irrigation, Paikand lost its importance and was left high and dry. Bukhara replaced Paikand as the principal city since it was situated where several canals branched from the river to irrigate fields. Although the large oasis had many villages, the founding of the city of Bukhara probably was little more than a century before the Muslims came.

The ruler called Abrui (or Aberzi, Abravi) has been identified as the last Hephtalite ruler of the area before conquest by the Turks by Markwart (1938, 148), although the name is not found elsewhere. It is probable that the information about the pre-Islamic history of the region is a conflation of several sources and not all necessarily relating to Bukhara. The settlement of Sogdians from Bukhara in Jamukat in present Kazakstan is quite plausible, since the establishment of trading colonies to the north and east began early. For an account of trade between the Sogdian oases in Central Asia and China see *Travels of Ibn Fad-lan* (Markus Wiener Publishers, 2005) with references.

The statement that the word jamuk meant a jewel in the language of Bukhara is interesting, for it may be related to the Russian word zhemchug, "pearl." The dynasty or family, which ruled the area around present Tashkent and to the north, was called Jamuk, which is recorded in Chinese texts as *Jao wu*.

The Turkic ruler who defeated and killed Abrui is called Shir-e Kishvar, a Persian translation of Turkic Il-Arslan, son of the great ruler Qara Jurin Turk. Various identifications have been proposed for the latter, and he may have been a ruler of the West Turkic Khaqanate, or even its founder Istemi, as suggested by Markwart (1938, p.147). Names here are not found elsewhere so it is difficult to identify the persons with historical figures. The story that nobles of the population of the oasis of Bukahra returned, and that Shir-e Kishvar built the city of Bukhara, is also not attested elsewhere, but it is likely that the site of the city was chosen sometime in the sixth century, not too long before the Arab conquests.

The Sogdian word for ruler xwabo was translated by the Persian word for "lord, master" *khudah*, not only in Narshakhi's work but elsewhere, so the king of Bukhara is mentioned as Bukhar Khudah in our text. There is no evidence elsewhere that the daughter of a ruler of China was sent to Bukhara as a bride for its ruler. It also questionable what the designation "Chin" meant, possibly only a local area in present Xinjiang. Chinese princesses were sent to nomadic rulers by the imperial courts of China, and it is conceivable that the ruler of Bukhara did receive such a bride, but this is only conjecture.

The statement that coins of pure silver were struck in Bukhara is hardly correct since Bukharan coins existed before this time, and the Muslim armies had not reached Bukhara in the time of the caliphate of Abu Bakr. Also Qutaiba ibn Muslim in Bukhara was after the time of the Umayyad caliph Mu'awiya, and the length of rule of Tughshada is questionable, unless we have a confusion of two rulers with the same name. Unfortunately this section of the book by another author is confusing when discussing the local rulers of Bukhara.

Narshakhi, however, is the author of the account of Khatun, the queen who ruled Bukhara on behalf of her infant son Tughshada when the Arabs first came to Bukhara. Acccording to Narshakhi she ruled wisely and successfully for fifteen years, but compare the ideas of Naymark. It should be noted that the *dihqans* were local nobility and not simply farmers as the word means today. A reception by the ruler, where two facing lines were formed by the subjects, was a time-honored practice in the Orient, and even today is found in Afghanistan.

The chapter on the villages of Bukhara is interesting inasmuch as it shows that the villages were not simply agricultural centers which provided food for the city, but were places of handicraft and manufacture, especially of textiles. For information about the textiles of the Bukharan oasis cf. (Riggisberger Berichte 2006.)

It is difficult to locate the villages mentioned by Narshakhi although some exist even today. Nun is Nur-ata; Tawais may be Kizil Tepe; Ramitin is Romitan; Farab is Firabr, and Ghujduvan exists today as Ghuzhdivan. I have tried to locate the ancient villages on a map but much is conjecture.

Likewise any attempt to locate the course of a canal mentioned in the book is hardly possible at the present since over the centuries many changes have occurred. In the chapter on coinage the figures on taxes are uncertain, but the statement that coins were struck with the ancient dies seems plausible. On the coinage of Bukhara see (Frye 1949–50).

Appendix I:
The Name and Antiquity of Bukhara

Richard N. Frye

Narshakhi tells us that Bukhara had many names (or appellations) but the name Bukhara is the best known. He does not give
an etymology for the name but other writers do. (Juvaini 1, 76),
an author of the 13th century writing in Persian, says that at the
time of its founding the name of Bukhara was Numijkath, and
"the derivation of the name Bukhara is from *bukhar*, which in the
language of the Magians is "the assembly place of knowledge."
This word is similar to that in the language of the idol-worshippers—the Uighurs and the Chinese (*lit.* Kathayans)— which
means "place of worship, i.e., the place of their idols is called
bukhar." An earlier author (al-Khwarizmi, 123,3) writing in
Arabic, was more informed when he wrote, "*bukhar* is a pagan
temple of the Hindus; *farxar* is a pagan temple of China and
Sogdiana." Many scholars concluded that the origin of the
name of the city was derived from the Indian word. Various ex-

planations of the name of the city may be found in (Tremblay
2004,122-5) where various etymologies are investigated. From
the Persian and Arabic sources, as well as Chinese, where older
An then becomes Nu-mi and finally Pu-ho, the name Bukhara is
late in time, perhaps the sixth century of our era. I suggest that
the name really is an appellative meaning "glorious" in Sogdian
fwx'r, which in turn is probably borrowed from Middle Persian
frxw with the same meaning. This, of course, is a popular designation, but many towns are known by similar designations such
as Roshan, Gulshan or Firdos in Iran.

Narshakhi tells us that the name of the city in Arabic is
Fakhira, again with a meaning similar to the above. It is not
stretching the imagination that Narshakhi, and others knew both
Sogdian and Arabic and saw the resemblance in both form and
meaning of the words in both languages. The designation could
have been applied to the oasis and then was used for the principal city. On the other hand one may save the derivation of the
name Bukhara from a *vihara* by postulating an ancient Bactrian
form of the Buddhist establishment *bohoro* which was established
on the future site of the city of Bukhara in the period when the
Kushans ruled the area. If the word should be found then this
explanation might take precedence over others.

This does not mean that there was no settlement on the
site of the future city of Bukhara, since, as noted above, a
village called Numijkath existed there. That name probably
was derived from the name of the river Zarafshan, formerly
called Nami or Namik. Less likely is a derivation from the
Sogdian word for the numeral nine, thus "ninth town" after
the model of Panjikent. The name Numijkath seems to have
been transferred to another village near the city of Bukhara,
when the latter became the center of the oasis and took the
name of the oasis. This may be compared to an earlier time
regarding the name of the province of Fars in Iran in the
time of the Achaemenids, when the tribal and then provincial
name Parsa was given to the royal site Parsa (Persepolis for
the Greeks). The same was the case of Bactria and its principal city Bactra or later Balkh.

Although it has been claimed that the city of Bukhara is at least 2,500 years old (Mankovskaya, 70) this is unlikely, even though ancient remains have been excavated in the vicinity of the city. There were many settlements in the oasis and the most important in ancient times was probably Paikand (Arabic: Baikand) since it was built on elevated ground where the deltas of the Zarafshan and Kashka rivers almost joined before being dissipated just short of reaching the amu Darya. Narshakhi also says that Paikand was older than Bukhara. There is no reason to doubt the information of Nishapuri in the book of Narshakhi on the creation of the city of Bukhara when he writes: "This place which is today Bukhara (formerly) was a swamp; part of it was a bed of reeds and part planted with trees and a meadow. Some places were such that no animal could find footing there, because the snows melted on the mountains of the districts near Samarqand and the water collected there. In the vicinity of Samarqand is a large valley (in which is a river called Masaf [Zarafshan]). A great quantity of water would collect in that river, and the water would dig away much earth and carry down much earth so these hollows would be filled . . . . The area which is Bukhara was filled and the land became level. The (river) became the great river of Sughd and the filled area became Bukhara."

There is no evidence that the Zarafshan River reached the Amu Darya in historical times, and the existence of swamps and lakes is almost certain. Ptolemy mentions an Oxian lake which could have been situated in the oasis of Bukhara, perhaps at the combined deltas of the Zarafshan and Kashka rivers. At an early date irrigation canals were created throughout the fertile oasis of Bukhara and the village of Numijkath stood at an area where the Zarafshan divided into several branches. This geographical advantage, as well as the ability of the ruler of the village to control the water for irrigation, enabled the rulers of the area to exercise successful rule over other villages in the oasis. Thus the ruler of Numijkath became the ruler of the entire oasis of Bukhara. I suggest that this happened little more than a century before the arrival of the Arabs.

Appendix II:

What Arabic and Persian Sources Tell Us about the Structure of Tenth-Century Bukhara

Heinz Gaube

In the tenth century, Bukhara was one of the most prominent cities in the Islamic world. It was the capital of the Samanids (874–999), a family of Persian origin, who gained quasi-independence from the caliphate of Baghdad in 874, and in the heyday of their power ruled over Transoxiana and eastern Iran down to Sistan in the south. The majority of them seem to have been very capable rulers. They exercised justice, cared for the rural population (as Narshakhi points out). They were involved in trade—even with Europe, as the thousands of Samanid coins found in the Baltic and Scandinavian countries testify. However, the main source of the government's income and investments was the slave trade. The Samanid territory was located on the northern and the eastern borderland between the *Dar al-Islam* and the *Dar al-Harb*, that is, the Islamic countries and the non-Islamic countries. The latter were a bountiful source of human resources. Thousands of Turks were stolen or bought from the lands of the infidels by the Samanids, used in their own state, or transported to the court in Baghdad where Turkish slave soldiers already played an important political role.

Trade, agriculture, and—most important—slaves were the economic basis of the Samanid state, and a healthy state creates or attracts creative minds. Thus it is not surprising that the Samanid realm generated scholars and artists, and they flourished. Two examples are Ibn Sina (Avicenna) (d. 1037), the most original philosopher of the Islamic world and teacher of medicine who surpassed Hippocrates and his successors and was more or less canonic for European medicine up to the eighteenth century, and al-Biruni (d. 1048), who can be considered the father of comparative religious sciences and ethnology in Islam. Both of them wrote in Arabic (for Ibn Sina a few Persian lines are also preserved), which up to the time of the Samanids was the only acceptable language of the pen in the Islamic world. But this too changed under the Samanids: after more than two centuries of Islamic rule over Iran, Persian was reborn as a written language. One of the viziers of the Samanids, Bal 'ami (d. 974), produced a Persian version of the Arabic chronicle of al-Tabari. Firdawsi (d. 1020), the author of the *Shahnamah*, the "Book of the Kings," was the real founder of new Persian literature. Many more personalities, in both literature and the sciences, could be named to prove Bukhara's importance in the Islamic world at that time.

The Written Sources

In the Samanid period, Arab rationalism, which had been fostered by the caliph al-Ma'mun (d. 833) led to the creation of a new scientific field, which we would now call "human geography" or social anthropology. Its founder was al-Balkhi (d. 934). As his name shows, he also came from Samanid territory. Unfortunately, his work, which consisted of maps and their descriptions, is not preserved. We only know of his method through the works of three of his successors: al-Istakhri (d. after 951), Ibn Hauqal (d. after 980), and al-Muqaddasl (d. after 985). The works of al-Istakhri and Ibn Hauqal are almost identical. It is hard to decide whether Ibn Hauqal simply copied most al-Istakhri's work or whether copyists intermingled their works at a later time. Differences do exist between the two, which proves that each of them did independent research. Which of the two had really seen what he described is difficult to determine. As far as Bukhara is concerned, al-Istakhri and Ibn Hauqal only differ in words and style, so the information they provide must be taken as a synoptic whole. The third in this group, al-Muqaddasi, never visited Bukhara, so his work is of less relevance to the questions we are dealing with here.

In addition to these authors of the tenth century is another, al-Narshakhi, a local historian of Bukhara who dedicated *History of Bukhara*, written in Arabic, to the Samanid Nuh b.Nasr in 934. In 1128 it was translated into Persian, and today only later abridged and "updated" versions are preserved. This means that all the information provided by this work does not necessarily relate to the tenth century.

Topography

After a general description of Bukhara, al-Istakhri and Ibn Hauqal remark, "In the whole of Khurasan and Transoxiana there is not one settlement with a higher building density than Bukhara, and with more people in relation to its area." Both start their description of the city by mentioning that Bukhara is the capital of Khurasan. Its name was Bumijkath. The city was located on a plain. Its houses were built close to each other using a half-timbering technique. Muqaddasi (280) comments that they were built in the same way as houses in Damascus, which is in fact true to this day. I have no plausible explanation for this. In other oasis towns we find that other techniques were and are used.

The Walls

The city and the area surrounding it were covered by palaces, gardens, small settlements, and residential quarters. The city itself had paved streets. The entire area was protected by a wall, which measured *12 farsakhs* by *12 farsakhs* (ca. 72 x 72 km). This wall is mentioned by Narshakhi as well, who says that its name was "Kanpirak." According to him, the wall was of pre-Islamic origin and restored in the early Islamic period. Inside the walls there was scarcely a spot that was not built upon or under cultivation. Remnants of this wall could still be seen in the fifties.

Inside the wall, which protected the oasis of Bukhara against nomads and sand from the nearby desert, was another wall measuring *1 farsakh* by 1 *farsakh*, i.e., ca. 6 × 6 km, which surrounded the city and its suburbs. This was definitely the predecessor of the wall, which is still visible in many places today. The city proper or inner city, the medina, was protected by a third strong wall. Remnants of this wall are also preserved, but information about both walls is confusing.

The Citadel

Outside the medina, but very close to it, was the citadel. Narshakhi attributes its construction to the legendary hero Siyavush. It is described as having been like a small medina or circumvallated town. Here the Samanid amirs of Khurasan resided. Within this citadel were also another fortress *(qal'a)* and the prison. Narshakhi's description is more explicit than those of al-Istakhri and Ibn Hauqal. He writes: "The fortress was the place of residence of rulers, amirs, and generals. It was also a prison and a chancellery; the castle [i.e., the fortress within the citadel] was the residence of the rulers." But this accumulation of functions for the citadel might refer to post-Samanid times. Narshakhi later wrote of the courts and bureaus of the officials at the *Registan* between the western gate of the citadel and the Ma'bad gate. Two gates led to the citadel, the Registan Gate in the west and the gate of the congregational mosque in the east; they were connected by a street. Interpreting this information poses no problem. There is no question that the *quhindiz* or *qal 'a* are identical with today's Ark. The Registan Gate still exists. It is the western gate of the Ark which leads to Registan Square. The gate of the congregational mosque opened to the east; it no longer exists. We may assume that the *qal'a* in the citadel was located to the southwest of the ark; there the only remnants of the amir's palatial quarters are preserved. This is suggested by its location adjacent to the wall of the Ark and the Registan Gate, a typical position for a *qal'a* in an Islamic medina, as al-Istakhri and Ibn Hauqal write of the Ark.

The prison, which many Western travelers of the nineteenth century describe in dreadful terms, might always have been located in the same spot as it was in the nineteenth century, near the passage leading from the Registan Gate to the palatial area of the nineteenth and earlier centuries. Today it is a museum.

Until 1920, the year of the "Bukharian revolutions," when the Ark was bombarded and destroyed, all the empty spaces around the present Ark were densely built up. We can probably locate the palatial areas of the Samanids and their officials there.

The Medina or Inner City

Our sources are not very systematic in their descriptions of the city. They jump between the inner city, the citadel, and the suburbs. One has the feeling that either al-Istakhri and Ibn Hauqal never visited Bukhara, or that if they did, they did not understand this type of city, which had little or nothing in common with the cities west of Transoxiana. The same can be said of al-Muqaddasi, who is even more unsystematic. And Narshakhi's information is that of an insider who does not bother to try to give an understandable description. The people he addressed in his book already knew what Bukhara was and what it looked like.

About the medina little is said by our authors. It was protected by a strong wall, it had no running water because of its elevation (the same is true of the citadel; it is still the case even today). It was densely built up with houses, because the *suqs* or bazaars were located in the suburbs. Seven gates led to the medina—or the *shahristan*, as Narshakhi's editors call it in Persian. Al-Istakhri (306) and Ibn Hauqal (483) give the following names for them:

Bab al-Madina; Bab al-Nur: Bab al-Hufra: Bab al-Hadid; Bab al-Quhindiz; Bab Bani Asad (Bab Mihr); and Bab Bani Sa 'd

Narshakhi and his Persian editors deal with the gates of the *shahristan* in the context of the division of the city between the Arabs and the " 'Ajams" after the Arab conquest of 708. They interweave their description of the gates with stories typical of Persian literature. But these will help us to learn a little more about the inner structure of the medina/*shahristan*. They also write of seven gates, which they identify as follows:

Dar Bazar; Dar Bam Sa 'd; Dar 'Ala; Dar Bani Asad (Muhra, or Mihr); Dar Kubriya (Frye, "Gate of the Citadel"); Dar Haqqrah; and Dar Naw.

These two lists and the Narshakhi text help us to understand the structure of the inner city of Samanid Bukhara.

If we look at a contour map of this inner city its form becomes quite obvious. It had a more or less square shape, and the possible location of gates can be also detected. There seems to have been one gate in the south, four in the west, one in the north, and one in the east. These gates can be easily identified with the gates given by al-Istakhri and Ibn Hauqal. They start in the south with the Bab al-Madma, then turn to the east to the Bab al-Naw, then north to the Bab al-Hufra. And after these gates they mention four gates in the west: the Bab al-Hadid, the Bab Quhindiz, the Bab Bani Asad and the Bab Bani Sa 'd.

Most of these gates can be identified with the gates mentioned by Narshakhi. But we have a problem with Narshakhi's list. He or his editors, seem to place a gate between the Ban' Sa 'd gate and the Bani Asad gate, the Dar 'Ala. If we look at the contour map of the inner city of Bukhara, it becomes quite obvious that there was no need for a gate between the Bani Sa 'd and the Bani Asad gates. A much more logical location would be further north at the Bab al-Hadid, following al-Istakhri and Ibn Hauqal. Al-Istakhri and Ibn Hauqal list the names of the gates in a counterclockwise direction, starting in the south, then moving to the east, north, and west; Narshakhi starts in the south and moves west, north, and east. The following correlation can be made:

Al-Istakhri/Ibn Hauqal: Babal-Madina; Bab Nur; Bab Hufra; Bab al-Hadid; Bab Quhindiz; Bab Bani Asad; Bab Bani Sa 'd.

Narshakhi: Dar Bazar; Dar Naw; Dar Haqqrah; Dar 'Ala; Dar Kubriya (Frye, Gate of the Citadel); Dar Bani Asad; Dar Bani Sa 'd.

The basic sequence of gates is given by the Bani Asad Gate, which led to the court of the amirs of Khurasan located at the Registan. The Quhindiz Gate faced the citadel; the Hufra/Haqqrah gate must have left the inner city to the north, because Narshakhi tells a long story relating this gate to the famous scholar Abu Hafs Kabir Bukhari whose tomb is to the northwest of the city (even Narshakhi places it near the Naw gate) and the Medina or Bazaar Gate which can only be located in the south, since Narshakhi relates that this was the only gate near a *bazaar.* Until the beginning of this century, the center of the *bazaar* of Bukhara was to the south of the medina.

Narshakhi's text is confused, but for general information concerning the inner city it is of some value. Where al-Istakhri and Ibn Hauqal deal with the inner city only in a few lines, Narshakhi provides a good deal of information in his chapter, "On the Division of the City between the Arabs and the Natives." In this chapter the gates are described, but there are many paraphrases, which the Arabic sources miss. Narshakhi starts by writing about the division of the inner city by Qutaiba Ibn Muslim after the Arab conquest in 708. The inner city was divided in two: half was given to the Arabs and half to the locals. The dividing line ran from the Gate of the Citadel to the Bab al-Nur. The part south of the inner city was given to the Arabs and the northern part was left to the locals. Evidence confirming this is that the names of the two gates in the south of the western part of the inner city bear the names of Arab tribes. Of one of them it is said that in pre-Islamic times it bore the name Mihr. The Great Mosque is located in this section as well.

Narshakhi also gives us the names of the two quarters in the south. The quarter to the left upon entering the city was called the "quarter of the rogues": it had a Christian church, which was later transformed, into a mosque. The quarter to the right was called the "quarter of the castles." "There was a castle in this quarter where the *dihqans* and the amirs of Bukhara used to live" (Frye). The quarter is bounded by the city wall on the south, where there was a produce market outside the wall and on the east, where there was the market of the pistachio sellers outside the wall. The northern boundary was formed by the street leading to the Naw/Nur Gate.

If we look at the location of the gates and streets connecting them, we see two overlapping patterns. The Medina gate and the Hufra/Haqqrah Gate as well as the Bani Asad/Mihr Gate and the Nur Gate are connected by more or less straight streets, which cross in the center. This is a typical pattern of some cities in Central Asia and eastern Iran (e.g., Merv, Samarqand, Herat, Bam). In the northwestern quarter of the inner city a similar pattern can be detected attached to the main axis at an angle of ca. 30 degrees. We may assume that this is the oldest part of the inner city of Bukhara, and in fact here and on the citadel excavations turned up evidence showing they both were founded in the third century B.C. In antiquity this small town in the northwest and the citadel were in some way sister towns. There is a conspicuous elevation in the northwestern corner of this quarter. There had been a prison in the pre-Russian period, and we might assume that here was the citadel of this small Seleucid-Bactrian-Kushan town, as there was a citadel within the citadel.

The first Great Mosque of Bukhara was built by Qutaiba Ibn Muslim in the citadel in 712. It must have been a small mosque. In 770 a new mosque was built between the citadel and the medina or *shahristan*. Narshakhi gives a detailed description of the building, which was later added to and rebuilt. In principle, the location of this mosque must have changed little between the eighth century and the fifteenth century when the present congregational mosque was built. This is also attested by the Kalyan minaret from 1127 next to the southeastern corner of the mosque.

The Rabad *or the Suburbs*

As far as the areas between the inner wall (the wall of the medina) and the outer wall of the city are concerned, our sources give us no further information. Narshakhi's information is confused and cannot be used as a basis for interpretation. After rereading them, only al-Istakhri and Ibn Hauqal make sense. They start in their abbreviated style of writing: "And the *rabad* has through streets *(durub)* and they are: Darb al-Maydan; Darb Ibrahim; Darb Riw; Darb Mardakhshan; Darb Kalabadh (these two roads led to Balkh); Darb Nawbahar; Darb Samarqand (which led to Samarqand and the rest of Transoxiana); Darb Baghashkur; Darb Ramamithana; Darb Jadasarun (which let to Khwarazm); and finally, Bab Ghashaj."

With his usual insight, W. Barthol'd concluded that these eleven *durub* are identical with the eleven gates in the outer wall of the Bukhara of his time. If we look at the map, he was, with perhaps one exception, correct. Eleven gates or streets mentioned by tenth century authors and eleven gates at the end of the nineteenth century cannot be a coincidence. Our authors use the same counterclockwise system of listing these gates/streets, starting in the southwest. Since there are clear coordinates given by the Samarqand Gate in the eastern section of the north, where the road to Samarqand begins, the Jadasarun Gate with the road leading to Khwarizm, and the Kalabadh and Nawbahar Gates with the road to Balkh. That means the gates of the tenth century correspond to the following gates of the nineteenth century:

Maydan=Qarakul	Samarqand=Samarqand
Ibrahim=Shaykh Djalal	Baghashkur=Imam
Riw=Namaz-gah	Ramithna=Uglan
Mardaqsha=Sallakhana	Jadasarun=Talipakh
Kalabadh=Qarshi	Ghashaj=Shirgiran
Nawbahar=Mazar	

If we look at [a] map from 1872, which for this purpose is preferable to modern maps, only the location of the Samarqand Gate is somehow strange because the main south-north axis runs into a wall. Otherwise a clear organizational system becomes apparent. The centers of the streets leaving the medina / *shahris-tan* are the Taq-i Talpaq Furushan, the Bab Madina or Dar Bazar of the inner city, and the Registan in the west of the citadel.

A last problem must be solved, for Barthol'd, it seems, misunderstood al-Istakhri and Ibn Hauqal. They write:

"In the middle of the suburbs in the direction *('ala)* of their bazaars are streets *(durub)* and they are: Bab al-Hadid; Bab Qantarat Hassan; Bab at the Mah mosque; Bab Ruhna; Gate at the palace of Abu Hisham al-Kinani; Gate at the Suwayqa; Bab Farjaq; Bab Darwaza; Bab Sikkat Mughan; and Inner Samarqand street."

First al-Istakhri and Ibn Hauqal write about the streets *(durub)*, then they give the names of gates, and end with "inner Samarqand street." How can we understand this? Barthol'd simply created another wall. This means that, in his opinion, Bukhara did not have three walls but four. But there was no fourth wall between the inner city and the wall around the suburbs. Thus this information must be interpreted some other way. The eleven gates correspond to the eleven streets on the first list. The "inner Samarqand street" gives us the solution. The gates mentioned were the gates of the bazaar that protected the bazaar from the suburbs. Following the system described in al-Istakhri and Ibn Hauqal we can start with the "inner Samarqand street" and proceed west.

Further on, our sources give a short account of the canals, which provided the city with water. It is a general description of the oasis of the Sughd River, the Zarafshan. Long, more detailed lists of canals are given later in the descriptions. I must admit that at this point I am not sure what this means. Old Russian and other old military maps, not all of which I have at my disposal, might be of help. Thus I shall not deal with this very important topic now. In another year, perhaps, I shall be able to give a coherent interpretation of this important information.

Appendix III:

The Size of Samanid Bukhara: A Note on Settlement Patterns in Early Islamic Mawarannahr

Aleksandr Naymark

The first scholar to discuss the topography of early Islamic Bukhara in detail was V. V. Bartol'd. In his book, *Turkestan down to the Mongol Invasion,* he suggested a reconstruction of the city's outline based entirely on the early Islamic sources. Many elements of his reconstruction have by now been universally accepted. Bartol'd's knowledge of the city itself, however, was rather limited: he had at that time never been to Bukhara and had no appropriate plan of the city at his disposal. As a result, his reconstruction took into consideration neither the actual topography of the site nor the microtoponymics of nineteenth century Bukhara. As a result Bartol'd equated the outline of the nineteenth century city with that of Samanid Bukhara. Although in later works he did not extensively comment on the

outer *rabad,* he did mention once that early Islamic writers did
not provide information on the distance between the gates of
the interior and the exterior walls, and that that prevented one
from understanding how the Capital status attained by Bukhara
affected the city's development. In the same work, however,
Bartol'd retained his earlier identifications of the gates of the
exterior *rabad* with the city gates of Mangite Bukhara. After visit-
ing Bukhara in 1920, Bartol'd modified his ideas about the city's
topography, but these revisions were not adequately reflected in
his scholarly writings.

In 1923, I.I. Umniakov published an article on the historical topography of early Bukhara. In it, he maintained the same
view put forward by Bartol'd that the outer *rabad* of the Samanid
city had approximately the same outline as that of the Mangite
city of the nineteenth century.

The first scholar to make extensive use of waqf documents in
the study of old city's topography was M. lu. Saidjanov. Unfortunately, I wasn't able to obtain a copy of his article in the United
States and know it only through several brief citations, which do
not allow me to make any judgment of what Saidjanov's idea of
the exterior borders of the Samanid city was.

In 1936, V. A. Shishkin published a small book on the archi-
tectural monuments of Bukhara, which, despite its conciseness,
holds a very important place in the history of the scholarly
research devoted to this city. Among other important considerations, it contains the first attempt to define the boundaries of
the Samanid city:

> Determining the outline and the size of the city in this
> epoch involves some significant complications. Neither
> Narshakhi nor the Arab geographers nor later authors
> provide any direct information on this question. Only by
> combining a large number of small discrete facts, mainly
> derived from the study of cemeteries, mazars, and other
> historical sites, can we define the boundaries of the 9th–
> 10th century city with the high degree of approximation,
> and [even this reconstruction] is not reliable for all areas.

The ancient cemeteries known to us Chashma-Ayyub, Khwajah Charshamba, Turki Jandi, Khwajah Bulgar, Khwajah Nur Abad, and Khwajah Sesaron were situated along the borders of the city, beyond the city wall. Each of them was situated next to one of the city gates. Thus, the city limits roughly corresponded to a broken line drawn from the eastern end of the cemetery Chashma-Ayyub to the cemetery Khwajah Gunjar and Khwajah Charshamba. The southern border went from the northeastern corner of the Khwajah Charshamba cemetery to the northern edge of the Turki-Jandi (green bazaar) cemetery, and from there it reached the Khwajah Bulgar cemetery and the locality of Kal-abad (where the madrasa, mosque, and mazar preserving this name are situated), which marked the southern and the eastern border. Then from Kal-abad, leaving the swampy lowland near the Kwajah Nur Abad cemetery to the north, [the border goes] toward the Awliye-i Kabir mazar (the site of the ancient tower of Ayyaran), and from there [it reaches] the southern edge of the Khwajah Sesaron cemetery and the Chashma-Ayyub cemetery. This is the most probable outline of the ancient wall of the rabad. Therefore, the city in Samanid times was still rather small in terms of territory and hardly occupied half of the area of the modern city.

In the late 1930's, L. I. Rempel, exiled to Bukhara, also worked on the historical topography of the city. His study was completed in 1940 in cooperation with M. S. Andreev's expedition to Bukhara, but was not published until 1962. The strength of Rempel's work was its set of maps, which included his reconstruction of the plan of early Islamic Bukhara. A series of reconstructions produced by V. A. Lavrov is to a large extent based on the materials of Bartol'd and Shishkin, and it lost its value as soon as better graphic materials were published.

In 1954, O. A. Sukhareva published an article devoted to the topography of pre-Mongol Bukhara, which was later developed into a chapter of her book on Bukharan cities. In both publications, Sukhareva introduced into the discussion the microtoponymics of nineteenth- and early-twentieth century Bukhara.

A thorough knowledge of the contemporary city allowed her to make much greater use of the *Kitab-i Mulla-zade* as a source for the city's topography than scholars before her. She also worked with *waqf* documents. Sukhareva disagreed with the method of reconstructing the city boundaries suggested by Shishkin. She pointed out that the dates of the death of saints who are known to be buried in some of the cemeteries are not necessarily the dates for the founding of these cemeteries—the saint could have been buried in an already existing cemetery. In other words, it is not possible to define the date of the city's boundaries marked by these cemeteries. Sukhareva also showed that there was a tradition of burying people inside the city and even in private yards. She referred both to ethnographic material and to passages describing this practice in *Tarikh-i Bukhara* and *Kitab-i Mullazade*. In other words, she showed that some of the cemeteries could have existed within the city wall. Sukhareva made no attempt to define the boundaries of the Samanid city, except for the northern border.

O. G. Bol'shakov included a discussion of the topography of early Islamic Bukhara in his general study of the Islamic Central Asian city. His reconstruction of the *rabad* walls is based on very important considerations:

> The transformation of Bukhara into the capital of the Samanid state gave a new push to the city's growth. By the end of the 10th century it became one of the largest cities of Central Asia. It seems improbable that the wall, which has been erected in the middle of the 9th century and encompassed Bukhara when it was a city of secondary importance, could surround a territory substantial enough for the unavoidable expansion of the city after it became a capital.

As a result he disagreed with the reconstruction of the city boundaries suggested by Shishkin: "If V. A. Shishkin has defined the borders of Bukhara correctly, one would then have to conclude [from them] that Bukhara did not grow very much between the middle of the ninth and the middle of the tenth century, after it became the capital of the state; Bukhara of the sixteenth century was twice as large as the city of the tenth century." In order to support his thesis, O. G. Bol'shakov utilized all the evidence available to him that could possibly be evidence for the expansion of the city during the Samanid epoch. Many of his specific observations and conjectures are very interesting, but the scarcity of sources makes the picture he drew seem doubtful. The reconstruction of the *rabad* wall in the west is based on the arbitrary drawing of the Naukanda canal. The position of the southern border was defined on the basis of the supposition that the Gate of Ibrahim could not be located to the south of Namazgah and to the north of Turki-Jandi. It is not clear, however, why Turki-Jandi is placed within the city walls with such conviction. The reconstruction of the eastern wall is based on the assumption that the large district of Kalabadh was situated in the city. This assumption, however, is not validated by the direct reading of the sources. The position of the northern wall is not really discussed.

E. A. Davidovich wrote an extensive review of Bol'shakov's work, where she put forward quite a few new solutions and introduced new material. The main achievement of this study with respect to Bukharan topography was the new interpretation of the interior *rabad*. As a starting point Davidovich used the very important conjecture of Bol'shakov that the *darbs* named after bridges should be situated near Shahrud. Further analysis of the evidence led her to the conclusion that the interior *rabad* was a territory on the eastern and southern sides of the city. The only *darb* of the interior *rabad, which she left to the west of the Shahristan,* was Darb-i Ahanin. Later G. A. Juraeva published materials, which located the Darb-i Ahanin beyond doubt on the southern side of the city. That confirmed the suggestion made by Davidovich that the in-

terior *rabad* was most probably a local addition to the city's
territory on the southern and eastern sides of the old *shahristan*. As for the city's size, Davidovich severely criticized most
of Bol'shakov's suggestions and concluded that not enough
data existed for such a reconstruction. She also pointed to
the fact that the growth of the city did not necessarily mean
territorial expansion, "There is also another important form
of growth represented by change of type and density of the
urban fabric." She found supporting evidence in the descriptions of al-Istakhri and al-Muqaddasi. This undoubtedly
correct assumption, however, is not necessarily applicable to
Samanid Bukhara. Though no houses dating to the Samanid
period have been excavated there, we know that the dwellings
in the city were mainly frame structures with walls erected
on the "cradle" principle. Frame construction is rarely raised
beyond the second story and never would have been more
than three stories high even in the most densely built-up city
centers of Central Asia. As far as we know, Sogdian cities of
the early eighth century were also very densely built up and
the majority of the buildings in them had two or even three
stories. In other words, there is no material to support the
statement that there was an increase in the density of the
urban fabric in Bukhara between the eighth and tenth centuries. Another explanation for the contradictions between city
size and the supposed development of city territories under
the Samanids was suggested by M. E. Masson in his extensive
review of Bol'shakov's work:

The actual official size of Bukhara did not exactly correspond to the territory encircled by the pre-Samanid wall of
the exterior *rabad* of the 9th century, as the wall with 11 gates
surrounding the inner quarters of Mangit Bukhara did not
define the size of the capital of the Bukharan Khanate. The
comment of al-Istakhri that Bukhara occupied the area of *farsakh* by a *half-farsakh)* should be understood as referring to the
area within the conventional administrative borders of the city,
rather than to the territory surrounded by the wall of the *rabad.*

Such an understanding of the size of the city territory, for which we also have examples from other cities in Central Asia, makes the comparative analysis of the size of Bukhara in different epochs ungrounded, if one takes into consideration only the territories surrounded by the exterior walls.

As this passage shows, Masson took the size of Bukhara *"farsakh by farsakh"* at face value. It is, however, one of those notorious round numbers, easily reduced by half in the Persian translation of al-Istakhri. Since later works do not say anything about the position of the walls of the exterior *rabad*, the problem remains unsolved, awaiting a "deep and objective study."

In terms of written sources one can expect new and interesting discoveries in waqf documents and other deeds of later periods. They may well solve the most intriguing problem of the "old *hisar*" *(hisar-i qadim)* and "new *hisar*" *(hisar-i jadid)* and show precisely what the boundaries of the territory described by these terms in the sixteenth and seventeenth centuries were. This would not, however, immediately solve the problem of the outside boundaries of Samanid Bukhara, because it is not clear which of the early city walls was referred to as *hisar-i qadim*. The problem could be solved by an archaeological study of one of the points described as the boundary of the "old *hisar*."

In the meantime a more general question about the forms of urban development was raised during discussions on the historical topography of Bukhara. The prospects of large-scale archaeological research in the living city of Bukhara do not look very promising. This forces us to turn for a solution to the general framework of urban development in Samanid Mawarannahr and in particular in the Zarafshan Valley. In other words, the study of the historical topography of Bukhara should be seen in the context of other cities, better known archaeologically. Comparison with other cities and the settlement pattern of the Samanid Mawarannahr would allow us to see which course of development is the most likely one and thus can help in understanding the sources.

Settlement Patterns in the Zarafshan Valley from the Fifth to the Eighth Century

Central Asian historians and archaeologists think of a city as being a densely built-up area surrounded by a wall. There are numerous examples, however, that show that this was not a universal rule in all parts of the ancient world, though up to now the majority of Central Asian cities of various epochs have conformed to this notion. In addition, there is abundant evidence that fortification did not play as significant a role in Samanid times as it did in other periods of Central Asian history. To illustrate this point one must turn to changes in the settlement patterns that took place in Mawarannahr during the preceding centuries. The pre-Islamic Soghdian towns in the Zarafshan Valley usually covered a relatively small area. Up to the seventh century, the walls of early medieval Samarqand, by far the largest city in the country, enclosed an area of about 70 hectares. As far as we can judge from cities with a clear historical topography the capitals of small principalities like Panjikant, Maimurg (Kuldor-tepe), Abgar (Durman-tepe), Kabudanjaket (Kurgan-tepe), and the secondary royal residence of Varakhsha and the self-governing city community of Baikand developed within an area of 20 hectares. The situation in Bukhara itself is unclear. Even the most optimistic reconstructions, however, keep the area of Bukhara within a 35-hectare limit.

A standard town had a citadel with a fortified city *(shahristan)* at its base. In some cases, however, the citadel and city formed two independent systems of fortification, as in Panjikant and Bukhara. *Shahristans* of the cities, which emerged or revived in the fifth century, were very often rectangular. Every new addition to the city's territory was fortified. In most cases the old wall behind the new fortification retained its military function, and the majority of Soghdian cities had more then one defense line at least in some directions.

Constricted by their own fortifications, Soghdian cities grew at the expense of inner territorial resources. One-story houses of the fifth century were replaced by two and three-story buildings in the sixth and seventh. In the course of the seventh century the open spaces between buildings and yards were eliminated, and by the early eighth century, the upper stories of Panjikant houses were extended on cantilevers over the streets, creating the phenomenon of fully covered lanes.

Suburban housing, in contrast, did not form a continuous fabric. Excavations and a detailed survey conducted by an expedition from the Moscow Museum of Oriental Art showed that the well-preserved environs of one large city—the remains of which are known as Durman-tepe—consisted of about a dozen castles and strongly built manor houses. A similar type of landscape was recorded around Kabudanjaket. A less explicit, but basically similar picture can be observed outside the walls of Panjikant and Paikand. Archaeological observations are supported by the story of Kashkathan in the *Tarikh-i Bukhara*, where merchants, displeased with having to share housing with the Arabs, moved to the suburbs and built castles surrounded by gardens and the houses of their dependants.

Rural settlements were enclosed by their own walls even when they were situated next to a town. In Sogdian Samarqand the majority of villages were dominated by the fortified castles of their overlords; in the Bukharan oasis, however, the proportion of fortified settlements without castles was also significant. In addition to compact villages, there were numerous free-standing castles and manors built to be capable of self-defense. The castles are comparable in size and richness of decoration to the dwellings of the nobility and merchants in the city, and in fact many of the latter were the urban residences of the landholding aristocracy. A peasant's household, however, was usually much smaller than a town commoner's dwelling.

The entire Bukharan oasis was surrounded by a long wall. A similar wall protected the area around Samarqand and a smaller one surrounded the arable lands of Nur. Despite their prominence as the masters of the Silk Road, the Soghdians did not leave us any structures along the caravan routes: the earliest caravanserais on desert roads belong to the Islamic period.

To conclude, the political and social conditions of Soghdian society were reflected in the settlement pattern in a very particular way. Life was concentrated inside the walls of the settlements and the expansion of the urban and rural structures went along with the building of extensive lines of fortification. In addition to the city and village walls the entire oasis was protected by long defense lines. In other words, Soghdian society, fragmented and exposed to constant pressure from the surrounding nomads, could not provide substantial security beyond these fortifications.

The Transitional Eighth Century

In the eighth century the Arab invasion began a chain of tragic events: constant wars lasted from Qutaiba's invasion in 706 to at least 739. They were followed by a series of revolts, the last of which, led by Muqanna', turned into a long peasant war. The times were especially bad for those who had previously had power and money. For example, none of the Bukhar-khudahs died in his own bed. Many nobles fled in attempts to escape the Arab rule and some were caught and eliminated. Many of the mansions of Panjikant were abandoned after the catastrophe of 722. It is very likely that numerous Soghdian castles abandoned in the eighth century were the estates of those families who had perished in rebellions and wars. There is little doubt that instability affected trade and the necessity to pay ransom money and tributes emptied the pockets of Soghdian merchants. Bukhara and Samarqand turned into strongholds of Arab rule and Islam. That drove old sovereigns from their palaces—the royal court of Samarqand moved to Ishtikhan, and by the middle of the eighth century most of the Bukhar-khudahs were living in Varakhsha. In some cases, the merchants, like the nobles, left the cities on religious and political grounds. The best example are the seven hundred families of Kashkathan. The loss of the nobility and rich merchants posed a severe problem for the cities, because they constituted the core stratum around which Soghdian cities were formed.

All these troubles, however, did not destroy city life. The economic potential accumulated by Soghdian society was so significant and trade relations with Soghdian colonies on the Silk Route were so strong that people were able to rebuild their ruined cities. "Qutaiba b. Muslim killed all those in the city of Baikand who were capable of fighting. He carried into captivity those who remained, so no one was left in Baikand, and it was ruined. The people of Baikand were merchants, and most of them had gone on trading expeditions to China and elsewhere. When they returned they searched for their children, women, and relatives, and they ransomed them from the Arabs and rebuilt Baikand as before." The revitalization of Panjikant dates to the 740's, made possible by the stabilization of the political situation after the treaty with Nasr b. Sayyar. Though there were apparently many fewer rich people among those who stayed back or returned, the city definitely did not cease to exist. Kh. G. Akhunbabaev traces the revitalization of a rich city quarter in Afrasiab to the same period.

A significant amount of archaeological material from the late eighth century has so far been accumulated only for Panjikant. According to these data, the city was abandoned some time after the Muqanna's revolt. Until recently, it was thought that the population of Panjikant left the old city in order to settle on another "cape" dominating the Zarafshan Valley. Several years ago, however, on the basis of excavations on the lower terrace of Zarafshan, N. F. Savvonidi suggested that the population left the old site of Panjikant for the lower terrace of Zarafshan, which was more suitable for agriculture. According to him, the former city dwellers turned into farmers. A century later, however, Arab geographers referred to Panjikant as one of the very few cities in the upper and middle courses of Zarafshan that was large enough to have a congregational mosque. It is very tempting to interpret this transformation of Panjikant as the only available example of the initial stage of the process, which led to the formation of a completely different settlement pattern by the second half of the ninth century. Unfortunately, the case of Panjikant has some unsettling peculiarities—for example, we do not know another city where the old town site was completely abandoned in the eighth-ninth century. In other words, we have very little material from the late eighth and early ninth century and can guess at the process of change only from the final results. These results, however, are striking: from at least the middle of the ninth century, we see a very different landscape on the same territory.

The Settlement Pattern of the Samanid Period

Samanid cities spilled over the walls and formed unfortified agglomerations covering many square kilometers of formerly rural territory. This makes any estimate of a city's size virtually impossible, for it is unclear where the urban area ended and the rural area began. There is no doubt, however, that the cities grew significantly compared to the previous period, though this expansion was not equal in all urban areas. Large administrative centers, like Bukhara and Samarqand, benefited a great deal from the new pattern of power distribution and grew disproportionally faster than many provincial cities like Baikand, which lagged behind. Bartol'd showed on the basis of early Islamic sources that the city citadels lost their significance and were sometimes even abandoned. Beginning with the Samanid period no new fortifications around *shahristans* were built, and old ones were often neglected. In Baikand, where the city walls had been constantly strengthened and restored during the last three centuries of the pre-Islamic period, in later times were repaired only once and only in one place. On the basis of the brickwork technique and a single piece of pottery from the mortar between the bricks the repair can be dated to the ninth century or later. The restoration was also very insignificant; no trace of it was found in another trench cutting at a distance of less than 20 meters from that point. To the best of my knowledge, no Samanid fortifications have been found in other Sogdian cities up to that date, with the exception of one repair of brickwork on the citadel wall at Afrasiab. The picture is striking compared with earlier periods, when constant repairs and enlargements led to the appearance of walls ten and more meters thick in practically every city.

There is also evidence that fortifications were neglected. A well (possibly for drainage) containing material from the tenth or early eleventh century was found, which had been dug into the body of the wall several meters from the point where the early Islamic brickwork was found in Baikand. Excavations from 1939 uncovered a pottery kiln from the middle of the tenth century, which was cut into its ruined southern wall. S. K. Kabanov discovered a drainage pit of the ninth century cutting through the wall at Varakhsha. This means that the fortifications of both cities were not functioning. This, together with the nearly complete absence of the fortifications in other cities, shows that city walls had lost their significance for the city dwellers in Mawarannahr.

Despite the numerous excavations of Samanid strata in different parts of Mawarannahr our knowledge of city dwellings is still rather limited. With very few exceptions, the absence of decoration in conjunction with their relatively small size suggests that they belonged to the poor stratum of the society. At the same time the urban fabric was less dense than it had been in the previous epoch: most of the ninth and tenth century city dwellings excavated in Mawarannahr had only one story, and inner courtyards became a common feature of urban housing once more. If this observation is correct, we may assume that land prices in the city were low. Low land prices could have resulted from a new phenomenon—the migration of many wealthy families to the suburbs. Samanid rulers moved out of the old citadels to live in palaces built in the *rabads* and beyond the city walls. Since the royal court was a large establishment, there is little doubt that the houses of courtiers and servants immediately sprang up around the garden palaces. We have a source for land value in the settlement of Kashkathan, which for the most part had been incorporated into the city. The estates of the "Magians became expensive because the rulers of Bukhara settled there and the followers and intimates of the sovereign wished to buy estates. So the price of one *juft* of these estates became 4,000 dirhams."

There were other significant changes in the suburbs also. Archaeologically the best preserved suburbs of a Samanid city are the ones around Varakhsha and in the Baikand oasis: production quarters formed relatively compact groups of buildings beyond the city walls; houses with large gardens stretched along the canals; and *ribats* were lined up along the main roads. By the end of the period sanctuaries with related complexes of buildings sprang up in the cemeteries. Written sources add bazaars to this list. Though we do not have a detailed description of the Bukharan environs, we know that they were similar to those in Varakhsha because Narshakhi states that "the *rabad* of Varakhsha is like that of Bukhara." The situation in the towns of the countryside is less clear, but similar to that observable in the suburban areas. Excavations conducted by the expedition of the Museum of Oriental Art on Talli-Pupa, a village with a castle situated four kilometers to the east of Varakhsha, showed that the early medieval wall of the settlement was neglected and dwellings dating from the ninth or tenth century built upon it. As a survey showed, freestanding houses appeared on the surrounding plain at approximately the same time. The rather significant tenth century settlement at Durman-tepe, the survivor of the earlier town, had no fortifications even on the citadel. The most impressive example, however, is provided by the oasis of Kum-Sovtan situated on the lower reaches of Kashka-darya in the Karshi steppe. A survey conducted by the Moscow museum expedition discovered there a large area with small separate houses scattered on the plain along the branches of the small canals, completely open to the surrounding steppe. Ancient oasis walls, which were still being repaired in the eighth and in the first half of the ninth century, were being completely neglected by the tenth. The idea behind this attitude is expressed in an anecdote told by Narshakhi: Isma'il Samani freed the people of Bukhara from the duty of restoring the walls by saying, "While I am alive, I am the wall of the district of Bukhara." (Chains of *ribats* stretched along the Central Asian deserts for hundreds of kilometers (from Merv to Amul and then to Khwarazm along the left bank of the Amu-darya; from Khwarazm along the right bank to Gugertly and then through the desert to Bukhara; from Bukhara to Karshi, etc.) Even secondary roads were often provisioned with *ribats* at important junctions. Cities situated at the points where main roads crossed the borders of an oasis developed large complex-es of *ribats*. It is worth mentioning that despite the widespread notion that *ribats* served a military function, none of the ar-chaeologically known Samanid *ribats* (unlike the *ribats* of the Qarakhanid and Khwarazmshah epochs) features any elements of real fortification. It is clear, then, that fortification and other considerations of security played no significant role in the settle-ment planning and urbandevelopment of the Samanid epoch. Apparently, under Samanid rule the people of Mawarannahr felt perfectly secure outside the fortification walls. The mighty bureaucratic state of the Samanids relied on the best army of the time, the Turkic guard corps, and did not want to invest in costly fortifications, which could be, and were at times, used against the supreme power by rebellious provincial governors and discontented city dwellers. Returning to the question of the size of Samanid Bukhara while keeping in mind the devel-opment of settlement patterns, it is clear, first of all, that the placement of the exterior wall of the city was no indication of its actual size. In fact, al-Muqaddasi says, after listing the *darbs* of the Bukharan exterior *rabad*, "Development, however, has gone beyond even these." The observations on the settlement patterns in the cities and villages of the Zarafshan Valley per-fectly match the history of the Bukharan ramparts as they are described in the *Tarikh-i Bukhara*. This chapter of local history was recorded by three or even four generations of writers, who carefully chronicled the history of Bukharan fortifications, but did not assign any wall construction to the Samanid period. On the contrary, the *Tarikh-i Bukhara* states that the fortification wall which had been erected just before the advent of Samanid rule in 849-50 was continuously repaired. The next large fortification undertaking mentioned in that work is the erection of the new *rabad* by the Qarakhanid Arslan-Khan Muhammad in the early twelfth century.

As to the exact position of the wall, it seems unlikely that it had encompassed a very large territory: there is no reason why the rather secondary provincial city of Bukhara would expand so much during the first half of the ninth century. The value of such general historical arguments, however, is doubtful; I hope that this discussion will at least have demonstrated this point.

Glossary

'adli — Arabic word for small coin.

Allahu akbar — "God is great," cry of Muslims.

amir — commander or governor.

dang — one-sixth of a dirham.

dhimmi — "people of the book," Jews, Christians and some-times Zoroastrians, with special tax on them.

dihqan — noble landowner, later a peasant.

dirham — unit of weight and coin, which varied from place to place, usually about $1.

dram — abbreviated form of dirham.

fatwa — a religious or juridical decree given by a mufti.

ghuruq — Turkic equivalent of Persian paradise, a royal hunting preseve.

juft — non-specific measure of land, theoretically the amount of land a pair of oxen might plow in a day.

khutba — sermon of loyalty to a ruler

maqsura — antechamber in a mosque for religious leader.

mihrab — niche in a mosque indicating direction of Mecca.

Minbar — pulpit in a mosque.

mithqal — a weight, which varied, an unknown amount in Bukhara at this time.

mufti — a magistrate who can issue fatwas.

parasang — farsakh in Persian. A measure of distance varies from three to six miles in different places.

pishiz — Persian word for a small coin.

qibla — direction towards Mecca for prayers.

ribat — a station or caravanserai, usually on the frontiers of the Islamic world.

tiraz — a fine cloth usually of silk.

rud — canal, river.

ruqu' — Muslim call to prayer.

Tir — fourth solar summer month of the Persians.

Tiraz — muslin- or silk-weaving establishment.

Bibliography

Frye, Richard N., 2001. "Bukhara Finale," in *Studies on Central Asian History in honor of Yuri Bregel*, ed. Devin DeWeese, Indiana University, Bloomington, Ind., pp.21–25.

Ibn Fadlan: Frye, Richard N., 2005. *Ibn Fadlan's Journey to Russia*, Markus Wiener Publishers, Princeton, N.J.

Juvaini, Ala'al-Din 'Ata Malik, 1912, 1916, 1937. *Tarikh-i Jahan-Gusha*, ed. M. Qazvini, GMS, 16, 3 vols.

Khwarizmi, Muh. ibn Yusuf, *Mafatih al-'ulum*, ed. G. van Vloten (Leiden, 1885), A.

Mankovskaya, 1991. *Bukhara, A Museum in the Open* (in Uzbek, Russian and English), Tashkent.

Naymark, Aleksandr, 2004. "The Coins of Khunak/Kanuk the Bukhar Khuda," from *Nisa to Niya, CIAA*, London.

Petruccioli, Attilio, ed. 1999. *Burkhar, The Myth and the Architecture*, The Aga Khan Program for Islamic Architecture, Massachusetts Institute of Technology, Cambridge.

Rezavi, Modarris, 1351/1973. *Tarikh-e Bukhara*, Tehran.

Riggisberger, Berichte: ed. Schorta, Regula, 2006. *Central Asian Textiles and Their Contexts in the Early Middle Ages*. Abegg-Stiftung, Zurich.

Tremblay, X., 2004. "La Toponymie de la Sogdiane etc." *Studia Iranica 33*, pp.113–149.

CPSIA information can be obtained
at www.ICGtesting.com
Printed in the USA
JSHW051556220722
28357JS00005B/75